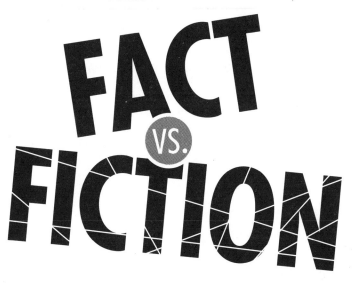

FACT VS. FICTION

Teaching Critical Thinking Skills
in the Age of Fake News

JENNIFER LAGARDE AND DARREN HUDGINS

International Society for Technology in Educ

PORTLAND, OREGON • ARLINGTON, VIRGINIA

Fact vs. Fiction: Teaching Critical Thinking Skills in the Age of Fake News

Jennifer LaGarde and Darren Hudgins

© 2018 International Society for Technology in Education

Acquisitions Editor: *Valerie Witte*
Development and Copy Editor: *Linda Laflamme*
Proofreader: *Corinne Gould*
Indexer: *Valerie Haynes Perry*
Book Design and Production: *Mayfly Design*
Cover Design: *Eddie Ouellette*

Library of Congress Cataloging-in-Publication Data Names: LaGarde, Jennifer, author. | Hudgins, Darren, author.
Title: Fact vs. fiction : teaching critical thinking skills in the age of fake news / Jennifer LaGarde and Darren Hudgins.
Other titles: Fact versus fiction
Description: First edition. | Portland, Oregon : International Society for Technology in Education, [2018] | Includes bibliographical references. | Identifiers: LCCN 2018051063 (print) | LCCN 2018055434 (ebook) | ISBN 9781564847027 (epub) | ISBN 9781564847010 (mobi) | ISBN 9781564847034 (pdf) | ISBN 9781564847041 (pbk.)
Subjects: LCSH: Critical thinking—Study and teaching. | Information literacy—Study and teaching. | Mass media—Study and teaching. | Fake news—Study and teaching.
Classification: LCC LB1590.3 (ebook) | LCC LB1590.3 .L34 2018 (print) | DDC 370.15/2—dc23
LC record available at https://lccn.loc.gov/2018051063

First Edition

ISBN: 9781564847041

Ebook version available

Printed in the United States of America

ISTE® is a registered trademark of the International Society for Technology in Education.

About ISTE

The International Society for Technology in Education (ISTE) is a nonprofit organization that works with the global education community to accelerate the use of technology to solve tough problems and inspire innovation. Our worldwide network believes in the potential technology holds to transform teaching and learning.

ISTE sets a bold vision for education transformation through the ISTE Standards, a framework for students, educators, administrators, coaches and computer science educators to rethink education and create innovative learning environments. ISTE hosts the annual ISTE Conference & Expo, one of the world's most influential edtech events. The organization's professional learning offerings include online courses, professional networks, year-round academies, peer-reviewed journals and other publications. ISTE is also the leading publisher of books focused on technology in education. For more information or to become an ISTE member, visit iste.org. Subscribe to ISTE's YouTube channel and connect with ISTE on Twitter, Facebook and LinkedIn.

Related ISTE Titles

Media Literacy in the K–12 Classroom, Second Edition, by Frank W. Baker

To see all books available from ISTE, please visit iste.org/resources.

About the Authors

Jennifer LaGarde has spent her entire adult life working in public education. She has served as a classroom teacher, a teacher-librarian, a digital teaching and learning specialist, district-level support staff, and a statewide leader as a consultant for both the North Carolina Department of Public Instruction and the Friday Institute for Instructional Innovation. Jennifer currently works with teachers, librarians, instructional technologists, instructional coaches, and both building- and district-level leaders around the world to develop innovative instructional practices. *Library Journal*, The American Association of School Librarians, *The New York Times*, and The Carnegie Corporation have recognized Jennifer's work. She's also the author of the award-winning blog *The Adventures of Library Girl*.

Darren Hudgins is CEO of Think | Do | Thrive, which helps educators, school leaders, districts, and school organizations build their culture, strengthen human capacity, and inspire the souls of social servants. He knows first-hand how difficult it is to cultivate and lead an environment of learning on a day-to-day basis as well as manage the rapid changes that are disrupting our society. Darren has spent his life fostering unique learning experiences in education on the front lines; he is a former secondary teacher, district coach, staff developer, speaker, facilitator, developer of technology integration programs, and youth coach. In addition to his work in schools, Darren has held roles including the Director of Instructional Technology for the nonprofit consortium Organization for Education Technology and Curriculum (OETC). There he had the pleasure of building a vast community of facilitators to help lead boutique professional development experiences (IntegratED Portland | AcceleratED Portland, SPARK, and Leading Schools, to name a few). He has facilitated keynotes for an array of schools, organizations, and parent advisory groups, and has conducted workshops on instructional strategies, leadership, capacity building, change management, CTE, STEAM, cohort/cadre models, and project-based learning across the United States. Darren has consulted for Future Ready Schools, Friday Institute for Educational Innovation, Nearpod, and various school districts. Darren is a Google Certified Innovator (#GMTV12) and holds an M.Ed. from Pacific University and dual Bachelor's degrees in Human Development and Social Sciences.

@dhudgins | dhudginspd@gmail.com

Acknowledgments

We very much want to thank everyone who made this book possible, although that would probably require an entire other book. That said, what follows is an incomplete list.

From Jennifer, a huge thanks to:

- ℺ My partner in crime, Darren, for always saying yes to my crazy ideas and for believing that we were worthy of this work. My life was made infinitely better the day you walked into it. *Wonder Twin powers—activate!* We did it, my friend. I'll take that steak dinner now.

- ℺ John and Jeannie for being an extra set of eyes when we needed them. You both make everything I do better!

- ℺ The educators who agreed to be interviewed for this book and who so willingly shared their stories with us. We owe you a huge debt of gratitude. Thank you, Scott, Arika, Len, Nikki, and Bill. Our work was strengthened by your stories.

- ℺ Our friends and families who supported us as we dedicated almost a year to this process. We couldn't have done this without you.

- ℺ The team at ISTE, including our editor Valerie Witte, who was patient and generous and who always believed in our ability to get this done! And to our copy editor Linda Laflamme, whose critical eye and gentle nudges moved us forward in the best way possible.

- All the educators out there who are currently on the front lines of the battle against misinformation. We need you and are so grateful for the work you do every day. Keep on!

From Darren:

- Jennifer, when you walked into my first presentation about fake news years ago, I was terrified. What a presence you carry as the most empowered media specialist I've ever met. Thanks for including me in this journey and using the cattle prod when it needed to be used. It's your tenacity that has helped you persevere in life, and it will be that tenacity that will help schools end this epidemic now and in the future.

- I, too, want to thank our educators and friends who helped us along the way.

- Lastly, thanks to ISTE for offering us this chance.

Dedication

To David, for always supporting this "writer on vocation" (not vacation). And to Sharron, for being "that teacher." This wouldn't have been written had it not been for the two of you.

—Jennifer

To Earl Craver (aka Cal Bolder) for putting the idea of a book in my mind. To my parents for giving me the opportunity to question things in life and grasp for the sunshine. Finally, to Jan, Braden, and Nolan for supporting Dad's passion to push others to critically think about the society they want to live in. I could not have done this without your support.

—Darren

Contents

Introduction

In the case of news, we should always wait for the sacrament of confirmation.

—Voltaire

On September 19, 2017, a devastating 7.1 magnitude earthquake struck Mexico, upending buildings, killing children in a school that was toppled, and sending people flooding into the streets of the capital, Mexico City. News of the devastation soon spread on social media, making the world aware of the peril facing central Mexico's citizens (Semple, Villegas, & Malkin, 2017). From their phones, tablets, and laptops, people watched the tragedy unfold and amplified the voices of survivors by sharing their stories, one Like, Retweet, and repost at a time.

Decades earlier in April of 1995, the bombing of the Alfred P. Murrah Federal Building in Oklahoma City, Oklahoma (History, 2009), similarly captured the attention of people all over the world. Unlike those who would follow the tragedy in Mexico City, however, those following the bombing and its aftermath had to stay glued to their televisions and radios, waiting for the news to be filtered through a media outlet, and then disseminated to the public in broadcast-sized chunks. (Jennifer remembers walking from work to join a crowd of people watching the story unfold on a large television at a corner deli.)

The Race to Be First

As the old saying goes "bad news travels fast," but today, all news travels faster than ever before. News feeds on social media sites coupled with push notifications sent directly to our phones makes news consumption something we have to actively opt *out* of now, rather than opt into. What's more, the advent of citizen journalism, that is to say the collection, circulation, and analysis of news and information by anyone with a mobile device, means that the general public often knows about the news, *before* the people in the news business do. This was certainly the case with the 2012 mass shooting at Colorado's Aurora Movie Theater, where witnesses were posting updates to social media well before news crews could even make it to the scene (Hawkins-Garr, 2013).

In 2017, following a terrorist attack at an Ariana Grande concert in Manchester, England, Britain's National Health Service (NHS) issued new guidelines related to the use of social media following major news events, such as terror attacks. In addition to warnings about the possible inaccuracy of information posted online during these events, the NHS also cautioned witnesses and/or victims to take extra care when sharing their own version of events with strangers online stating, "people will use your information for their own ends and when you're in the heat of the moment you may say more than you intend or later regret" (Silver, 2017). First person accounts shared on social media as the news events happen are the new primary sources of our time. But like all first person accounts, they represent only a single view of what are often complex situations. Journalists are trained to put these stories in context as part of a greater whole. But often that analysis, which takes time to build, isn't as emotionally compelling as a series of live Tweets from someone watching the event unfold. As the goal of breaking a story first has inched ahead of the goal of reporting a story most accurately, both intentional and unintentional errors have become commonplace in what we consume as news.

This rush to be first on the scene, along with all of the tactics journalists (both traditional and citizen alike) employ to ensure theirs is the story we click on, may also shed some light on why intentionally fake news stories spread faster on the internet than legitimate ones do. In the March 9, 2018 issue of *Science*, a team from the Massachusetts Institute of Technology (MIT) shared its analysis of over 126,000 news stories Tweeted by over 3 million users. The team found that on average, "it took the truth about six times as long as falsehood to reach 1,500 people" (Fox, 2018). They say that the truth is often stranger than fiction, but apparently it's not compelling enough to be shared as quickly. All of which brings us back to Mexico City in 2017.

The Earthquake and Aftershock

In the days after the earthquake that ultimately killed 369 people in central Mexico, people remained captivated by the coverage as events unfolded. But for at least a day and a half, the devastation and rising death toll were not the focus of all that attention, rather the world was united in following a single hashtag: *#frida*. The series of events behind the hashtag was well documented.

First, the Enrique Rébsamen school collapsed on that Tuesday, September 19, when a 7.1-magnitude earthquake hit Mexico City. People rushed to pull injured children from the school, but hope soon dwindled (Specia, 2017). By evening of the next day the military, the police, and local volunteers had been digging for more than 24 hours, but reports emerged of a girl who was alive inside the rubble (Muliany, 2017). Soon attention swirled around reports that a 12-year-old girl was trapped in the rubble of a collapsed elementary school as rescuers rushed to save her (Argen, 2017). It wasn't long before television cameras fixed their attention on the frantic rescue operations. Tidbits of information about the child, who some began to identify as Frida, trickled out. Some reported that she was with five other children, others that she had spoken to rescuers and wiggled her fingers, and still others that she had been sent water.

Danielle Dithurbide, reporting for Televisa, Mexico City's largest news network, said that rescuers had told her that a 12-year-old girl was trapped, and that she had been found using a thermal scanner. Rescue teams, she told viewers, had made contact with the child whose name was Frida Sofia. Rescuers were withholding the last name, the reporter said. Later that evening, Ms. Dithurbide interviewed rescuers on camera who spoke of a child trapped alive in the building. In one interview, a man who identified himself only as Artemio and as an "electrician and rescuer" told her that he had heard the voice of a girl.

"Yes, some very faint voices of a girl, apparently called Sofi," Artemio said. "I asked, 'Your name?' She said, 'Sofi, Sofi'" (Noticieros Televisacom, 2017).

In the early hours of Thursday, September 21, the Associated Press (AP) quoted another rescue worker with a similar story. *The New York Times,* among other news organizations, published the AP report: "Rescue worker Raul Rodrigo Hernandez Ayala came out from the site Wednesday night and said that 'the girl is alive, she has vital signs,'" and that "five more children had been located alive. 'There is a basement where they found children.'" The report went on to state, "Helmeted workers spotted the girl buried in the debris early Wednesday and shouted to her to move her hand if she could hear. She did, and a rescue dog was sent inside to confirm she was alive. One rescuer told local media he had talked to the girl, who said her name was Frida" (Associated Press, 2017).

Here's what happened next:

- #Frida trended on Twitter (Agren, 2017).
- A military search-and-rescue dog also named Frida was employed to work at the site (Volmiero, 2017).
- The story of Frida grew as more news outlets reported the information of the rescue efforts, one after another (Noel, 2017).
- Millions of people all over the world followed the story wondering if Frida would be rescued and if there would be hope at the end of this terrible story.

But, of course, she never was, because, as it turns out, there was never a girl trapped in the rubble. Frida Sofia never existed (Mullany, 2017).

As we were researching *Fact vs. Fiction*, the story of Frida Sofia kept rising to the surface as an example of how, collectively, people get caught up in narratives. And we couldn't help but wonder:

CHAPTER ①

Facts Are So 2015:
Why This Book? Why Now?

post-truth /ˌpəʊs(t)ˈtruːθ/

adjective

Relating to or denoting circumstances in which objective facts are less influential in shaping public opinion than appeals to emotion and personal belief.

"in this era of post-truth politics, it's easy to cherry-pick data and come to whatever conclusion you desire"

"some commentators have observed that we are living in a post-truth age."
("Oxford Living Dictionaries," n.d.)

Every year, Oxford Dictionaries selects a word as Word of the Year. In addition to being a word that was used extensively during the previous 365 days, the chosen word also reflects the "mood and preoccupations" of the passing year. In 2016, that word was *post-truth*. According to the editorial staff, research conducted by Oxford Dictionaries revealed that use of the word had increased by approximately 2,000% over its usage in 2015 ("Word of the Year," 2016).

And yet, unlike previous choices for Word of the Year, the selection of *post-truth* seemed rooted as much in the future as it was in the year that had just passed. Indeed, in the time since Oxford Dictionaries declared that our vocabulary had expanded to encompass the new world in which facts no longer seemed to matter, our concern and befuddlement over the spread of misinformation has continued to grow.

The Edelman Trust Barometer is an annual survey of 28 countries around the world that offers a glimpse into the amount of trust people place in their countries' governments, media, businesses, and so on. In the 2018 survey, 59% of respondents said they did not trust what they saw represented as news in the media, and 63% said they did not believe the average person had the skills to discern real news stories from those that were fake. As Stephen Kehoe, global chair of reputation at Edelman, told CNBC when the survey data was released, "In a world where facts are under siege, credentialed sources are proving more important than ever. There are credibility problems for both platforms and sources. People's trust in them is collapsing." His assertion was supported by the data: 65% of those surveyed included social media sites and search engines as their news source, but trust in those platforms decreased in 21 of the 28 countries Edelman surveyed (Edelman, 2018).

In the U.S. in particular, this distrust extended to government agencies as well, with only 33% of respondents indicating they trusted government resources. This erosion of trust by Americans in both their government and a free press, one of the hallmarks of the country's democracy, was not lost on those responsible for collecting this data, whose summary of the results included this call to arms:

> It is no exaggeration to state that the U.S. has reached a point of crisis that should provoke every leader, in government, business, or civil sector, into urgent action. Inertia is not an option, and neither is silence. The public's confidence in the traditional structures of American leadership is now fully undermined and has been replaced with a strong sense of fear, uncertainty and disillusionment. (Edelman, 2018)

And so, we find ourselves living a post-truth world, where "alternative facts" and "fake news" dominate our discussions and compete, often winning, against once authoritative and mainstream information sources. Why is this happening? Naturally, the answer is complex and varies depending on whom you ask. It's tempting, of course, to blame technology, for, indeed, the internet and the penetration of smartphones into our everyday lives have amplified the problem. (In later chapters, we'll explore how technology hastened the advent of an entire industry devoted to deception, while also offering some of the best tools available to help us dig ourselves out of this hole.) It's also tempting to point the finger at an increasingly ignorant populace and to long for the "good old days" when people were smarter and more virtuous, or to view our ability to be fooled by increasingly slick propaganda as a personal failing. For now, however, rather than focusing on how we got here, let's consider the consequences of this strange and uniquely 21st-century journey.

Nothing You Can Say Will Convince Me Otherwise

In the days leading up to the 2016 U.S. presidential election, many news organizations spent time interviewing likely voters, asking them why they'd chosen to cast their votes for a specific candidate. Jennifer remembers watching one such interview in which a decided voter passionately cited a story that already had been debunked numerous times. The story linked former Secretary of State and presidential candidate Hillary Clinton to a child trafficking ring. When the reporter confronted the voter with examples of how that story had been proven false, the voter simply dug in rather than consider the reporter's view and said, "nothing you can say will convince me otherwise." When faced with empirical evidence, this voter chose to put her faith in her own beliefs. What's more, she's not alone.

Numerous psychological studies, over several decades, have concluded that when faced with facts that dispute deeply held beliefs, people overwhelmingly search for ways to discredit those facts while clinging to the personal narratives that support the things they believe to be true (Kolbert, 2017). Couple this with a political climate of near toxic polarization, and you're left with a recipe that spells disaster for logic and reason. But it doesn't end there. In addition to being unwilling to consider explanations that do not support our own biases, we're also far more willing to share information that *does* support our beliefs—without vetting that information for accuracy.

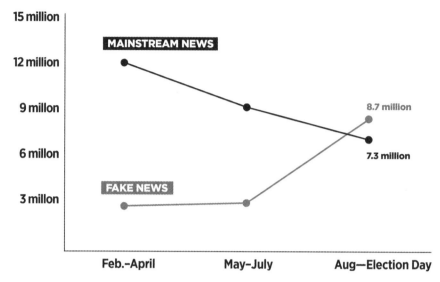

Total Facebook Engagements for Top 20 Election Stories

MAINSTREAM NEWS

FAKE NEWS

8.7 million

7.3 million

15 million
12 million
9 million
6 million
3 millon

Feb.–April   May–July   Aug—Election Day

ENGAGEMENT REFERS TO THE TOTAL NUMBER OF SHARES, REACTIONS, AND COMMENTS
FOR A PIECE OF CONTENT ON FACEBOOK SOURCE: FACEBOOK DATA VIA BUZZSUMO

Figure 1.1 Despite the fact that most people consider themselves savvy at detecting fake news, an analysis by BuzzFeed revealed that Facebook users shared more fake news stories than real ones in the run up to the 2016 U.S. presidential election.

In November 2016, an analysis conducted by the site BuzzFeed News (Figure 1.1) found that the top fake election news stories (stories that were proved to be false by independent analysis) generated more total engagements (Likes and shares) on Facebook than the top election stories from nineteen major news outlets combined (Silverman, 2016).

What's more, because social media outlets, such as Facebook and Twitter, allow users to unfollow people whose postings contradict their own beliefs without ever notifying the other people that they've been unfollowed, there's no social consequence for removing differing opinions from your information stream. Without the risk of an awkward, potentially embarrassing, or even confrontational conversation, we can eliminate the inconvenience of contradictory opinions from our online lives with just a few clicks.

Of course, this happens, to some degree, without us having to be complicit at all. In 2018, Facebook CEO, Mark Zuckerberg was called before the U.S. Congress to testify about the revelation that the private data-collection company Cambridge Analytica had gathered information from up to 87 million of Facebook's users without their knowledge. In total, Zuckerberg testified for over ten hours and faced nearly 600 questions, this one from Republican Senator Roger Wicker: "There have been reports that Facebook can track users' internet browsing history even after that user has logged off of the Facebook platform. Can you confirm whether or not this is true?" Although the Facebook CEO didn't answer the question directly, instead promising to have his team get back to the senator later, he did mention that cookies (the bits of information that web servers collect, store, and pass to your browser as you visit different sites on the internet) may make that possible.

In his 2011 book and corresponding TED Talk, "The Filter Bubble: What the Internet Is Hiding from You," Eli Pariser warns us all about how the internet uses the data it collects while we surf the web to not only sell us things, but also to hide information from us that we find uncomfortable or that doesn't align with the opinions our clicks and Likes seem to support. Over the years, these algorithms have become more sophisticated and better at doing their job, which is to tailor the internet experience to a specific user's interests and beliefs. As a result, retail companies are better equipped to show us ads for things we might actually purchase, and companies like Cambridge Analytica can use a "personality quiz" to identify potentially sympathetic voters who may be worth targeting by a specific political party or candidate. At the same time, this increased sophistication also means that we are far less frequently confronted by ideas or viewpoints that don't match our own, making us less and less capable of having a reasonable discussion involving divergent points of view. In the end, whether or not we *actively* participate in our own insulation from ideas we disagree with, the internet has evolved to help this process along.

So what does this have to do with fake news?

A 2017 poll conducted by the Pew Research Center recorded that 67% of Americans get at least some of their news from social media. The same poll indicated that news consumption via Facebook, Twitter, YouTube, Snapchat, and other social media sites was on the rise in demographic groups such as older people, non-Whites, and those with limited education, who have historically relied on more traditional sources of information (Shearer & Gottfried, 2017). Although these trends clearly present a problem when taken in the context of how our social media feeds are both intentionally and unintentionally filtered to support our own biases, they also present an opportunity for political parties and those whose personal and professional goals center around getting candidates elected. With more people turning to their own, increasingly biased, social media feeds for news, those feeds become fertile ground for planting stories that look a lot like legitimate news but don't require the same kind of vetting that traditional journalism relies on.

Many people in the public eye, including politicians at the highest level of the U.S. government, have further capitalized on this hamster wheel of bias and disinformation. Rather than railing against the notion of fake news and seeking to support the validity of their own opinions or policies with facts and data, those in power use the term as a label with which to discredit those who disagree with them or whose data contradicts theirs. Indeed, as of January 2018, President Trump had been recorded using the term *fake news* to describe traditional news outlets over 400 times since his inauguration (Stelter, 2018). Intentional or not, one consequence of this very public repetition of the term makes every successive use less effective than the last. Put another way, as the Liar's Paradox goes: "When everything is false, nothing is false." The more we consider news to be suspect, the more all news sources, regardless of their journalistic integrity and editorial oversight, become equally suspect as well. For those who rely on disinformation to further an agenda, this seems like a preferable outcome.

Where Do Educators Fit in a Post-Truth World?

Early in George Lucas' *Star Wars* (1977), Imperial forces capture a rebel ship. While listening to the ominous explosions and awaiting the inevitable arrival of the white-armored stormtroopers to spill into the hallway where they stand, the universe's most erudite droid, C-3PO, turns to his companion

R2-D2 and says simply, "We're doomed." We know how he feels. It's tempting to look at the situation we've found ourselves in and feel hopeless. But as two people who have spent a lot of time studying the phenomenon of fake news, we are (cautiously) optimistic. What's more, we believe that, in the end, educators hold the keys to getting us out of this mess.

In a world in which facts are considered passé and an entire industry exists to deceive information consumers, the abilities to discern fact from fiction and to respond productively to those who counter data with belief are critical skills. Although the delivery methods have changed and a focus on standardized testing in math and English have reduced instructional emphasis on literacy, history, and civics, educators have always been information conduits and experts at helping students gain strategies to locate reliable sources. As the amount of information being generated has increased exponentially and the ways in which we access it have become less regulated, we all have to ask ourselves, "Are average educators prepared to shift from teaching basic information literacy to being fierce defenders of truth?"

We think so. In fact, we see skilled teachers as the kryptonite against fake news and the purveyors of a better democracy. In the pages ahead, we hope to further unpack the challenges before us, outline ways for educators to help their students become smarter consumers of information than we have proven to be, and highlight examples in which practitioners are already leading the way for us.

Chapter 1

1. What's your why? In this chapter we shared some of the reasons why we felt a sense of urgency to write this book. What is your current motivation for wanting to help your students grow as information consumers and critical thinkers in the age of fake news?

2. Think about all the information presented in this chapter and take a minute to identify which pieces are, to you, the most urgent. Now think about your school or district. With whom would you most like to have a conversation about the information you prioritized? What would that conversation look like?

3. Tweet us! Yay! Your school has decided to hold a monthly Twitter chat aimed at parents and other community members. And there's more great news! This month the topic is media literacy. What are some Tweets you'd share on the night of the chat to help families better understand the phenomenon of fake news?

actual facts about battles and legislation with the fake details. Franklin sent his fake supplement to the *Independent Chronicle* first to respected friends in communities throughout the colonies, so that *they* could share it with others, adding *multiple source points* of the information—social media colonial style. He made sure to include some fake *eye witness accounts*, and of course, the horrific imagery of fellow colonists being brutalized by Native Americans, depicted as savages, created an *emotional and psychological investment* on the part of readers.

Sound familiar? Although the contents of the two stories are very different, the components that cause people to believe the false information contained in each are the same. This is important, because although it's tempting to look at fake news as an exclusively 21st-century phenomenon, doing so also allows us to lay the blame for the way it affects us as human beings (which we'll look at in more depth later) at the foot of the technology, which is both unfair and unwise. Technology has had a great impact on the speed by which fake news travels as well as on the expanse of its reach, but the reasons why people concoct it, and the reasons why we continue to believe it, remain largely unchanged.

In short, the problem isn't the technology, it's us. Or at least our brains. And it's not because we're stupid or don't have the skills to parse false information from what's true. Rather,

> in an era when the average American spends 24 hours each week online—when we're always juggling inboxes and feeds and alerts—it's easy to feel like we don't have time to read anything but headlines. We are social animals, and the desire for Likes can supersede a latent feeling that a story seems dicey. Political convictions lead us to lazy thinking. But there's an even more fundamental impulse at play: our innate desire for an easy answer. (Steinmetz, 2018)

The Psychology Behind Fake News

In the 1960s, British psychologist Peter Wason conducted a series of experiments to show how the brain processes information within the context of a preexisting belief. Essentially, here's how the experiment worked: Subjects were told by the person conducting the experiment (the presenter) that they would be given a set of three numbers which conformed to a simple rule that the presenter had in mind. Each subject was instructed to write down an initial hypothesis about the rule based on the supplied number set. If the presenter offered the number set "2, 4, 6," for example, a subject might write down "a set of three even numbers" as the hypothesis. Subjects were then invited to submit additional number sets of three to help them determine the presenter's rule. No matter how many sets they guessed, the presenter would then state whether the numbers conformed to the rule or not. Once a subject thought he or she had figured out the rule, that person could ask the presenter if the solution was correct (Explorable.com, 2010).

That's when things got interesting.

Regardless of how many number sets they submitted, the majority of subjects were wrong when they shared their hypotheses with the presenter. Why? Because in most cases, once a subject had written down his or her hypothesis, the person submitted only number sets that *confirmed* that belief. For example, if the hypothesis for "2, 4, 6" was "a set of three even numbers," the majority of subjects submitted only number sets containing three even numbers. Rather than testing their original hypothesis about the rule by naming sets that could prove it wrong, they sought only to confirm their existing beliefs. (If you want see a version of this experiment in action, check out the video at bit.ly/2vPSxcF.)

This series of experiments is the source of the term *confirmation bias*, or the idea that our brains naturally seek out information that confirms what we already believe to be true. The related term *implicit bias* refers to how our existing biases and stereotypes affect our understanding, actions, and decisions in an unconscious manner. Both terms help us understand why we are so prone to believe some examples of false information, while easily dismissing those that conflict with our beliefs. Conversely, it also explains why those who create fake news find it so easy to develop patterns that work. So, what can we do? Be aware of our biases, for a start.

For example, both Darren and Jennifer are coffee aficionados who start (and often end) their days with a mug in hand. Given this bias, we are both prone to believe studies claiming the health benefits of coffee, while putting less stock in those that highlight the risks. By being aware of our bias in this area, however, we can use that knowledge to be more critical consumers of information around this topic.

Exercising such awareness of bias requires daily practice—not just for us, but for our students, as well. What's more, the psychology behind fake news is not often a component of traditional approaches to media literacy. But perhaps it should be taught alongside the traditional strategies for media literacy.

The Frontlines: Teaching Media Literacy

As early as 1995, Alan November tackled media literacy in an article titled "Teaching Zack to Think" which "focused on teaching students techniques that would allow them to search with more purpose" (November & Mull, 2012). In 2013, reflecting on how the online landscape had changed in the intervening decades, November expanded his advice on how to "prepare our students to make meaning from the overwhelming amount of information at their fingertips." Teachers need to go beyond instilling good searching habits, he explained:

> This skill, while still important, is only one of three pillars we believe are now essential to be Web literate. These three pillars are...
>
> 1. *Purposeful search*: Using advanced search techniques to narrow the scope and raise the quality of information found on the Web.
> 2. *Effective organization and collaboration*: Being able to organize all of this information into a comprehensive and growing library of personal knowledge.
> 3. *Sharing and making sense of information*: Sharing what we find and what we learn with the world, and using the knowledge of others to help us make more sense of it all. (November & Mull, 2012)

Many schools use November's three pillars as the foundation for how they teach media literacy in the context of research. Some, too, enlist the help of the elusive Pacific Northwest Tree Octopus. In 1998, Lyle Zapato took to the internet on a mission to save this "endangered species" and created an entire website dedicated to the tree-dwelling octopod at https://zapatopi .net/treeoctopus. Despite offering a robust array of resources proving the animal's existence, everything on the site is false. This hoax website remains a popular resource for teachers who use it to help students spot fake sites on the internet, as well as help them exercise their skills of sharing and making sense of information. By comparing what they know about geography and biology to what they see on the site, young students, in particular, can discover that even when the information they see online looks credible, all sources of information should be evaluated to determine whether or not they hold up to scrutiny.

Another commonly used media literacy tool is the CRAAP Test (Figure 2.2). Created in 2010 by the Meriam Library of California State University, Chico, California, the five questions of the test are a go-to protocol for students (especially in middle school) to employ when trying to determine the credibility of sources online.

Clearly, teachers haven't been ignoring media literacy and the needs for our education system to help students think. But if these strategies and tools have been truly effective, why do we have a populace that increasingly believes whatever they see online?

The answer to this question is complex, and we'll explore some strategies for changing these outcomes in the chapters that follow. However, one thing we do know is that civics and social studies classes have historically been the places where students have explored the idea of propaganda, the role of the press, and how the two have been used throughout history for nefarious purposes.

Unfortunately, since the implementation of No Child Left Behind (NCLB) and an increased emphasis on STEM-related testing, coupled with the testing-driven prioritization of subjects such as English, science, and math, along with growing opportunities for remediation in these subjects being

CHAPTER 3

Fake News in an Exponential World

In November of 2016, *The New Yorker* ran a political cartoon that in many ways summed up the information landscape at the time (Figure 3.1). In it, the host of a game show called *Facts Don't Matter* informs a contestant, Jeannie, that although her answer was correct, the winner of that round was actually her competitor Kevin, who "shouted his incorrect answer over yours, so he gets the points" (Dator, 2016). The single-frame, sardonic, black-and-white drawing captured and acknowledged an uncomfortable truth: We have a problem.

Undeniably, the term *fake news* has called attention to the need for media literacy in a way that nothing else has before. At the same time, however, the phrase itself is an oversimplification of a complex and rapidly evolving problem. Implying that information falls into one of two categories—true or false—denies the subtleties within the false narratives that are being created to fool us, while doing nothing to address the reality that *how* we get our news may also be contributing to the dulling of our ability to discern what's there to inform versus what's been put in front of us to entertain, influence, or encourage us to consume. In this chapter, we'll unpack the nuances of fake news and how the ways we consume information make it easier to deceive us.

All the News That's Fit to Post: A New Media Landscape

As we mentioned in Chapter 1, as social media has evolved and become more pervasive, an increasing number of Americans have come to view these tools as having uses beyond just reconnecting with old friends and sharing filtered

Figure 3.1 This cartoon was shared countless times on social media as an expression of our collective frustration, with many people asking some version of the question: So, what do we do now?

photos of their favorite meals. Indeed, according to a 2017 survey conducted by the Pew Research Center, two-thirds of Americans (67%) report getting at least some news on social media. What's more, this growth was driven by significant increases among older Americans, which (coincidentally) is also the demographic representing the highest levels of voter turnout in both the U.S. general and midterm elections (File, 2017). According to Pew researchers, "For the first time in Pew Research Center surveys, more than half (55%) of Americans ages 50 and older report getting news on social media sites, a 10-percentage-point jump from 2016" (Bialik, 2017). We'll dig a little deeper into where our students get their news shortly. In the meantime, however, if we agree that parents and guardians are most influential in helping young people develop values and points of view, it is worth noting that much of what our students hear at home in relationship to news and politics is now more greatly influenced by social media than ever. And as we discussed in Chapter 1, much of what is being shared on social media in the name of news turns out to be fake.

Social media news user profiles

Social media news user profiles

% of each social media site's news users who are ...

	Facebook	YouTube	Twitter	Instagram	Snapchat	LinkedIn
Male	38%	55%	53%	40%	38%	56%
Female	62	45	47	60	62	44
Ages 18-29	25	36	28	51	82	14
30-49	40	34	43	36	15	50
50-64	24	19	21	11	3	25
65+	11	11	6	2	<1	11
High school or less	35	33	22	39	35	12
Some college	33	37	33	36	39	28
College+	32	30	45	25	26	59
White	65	49	59	32	27	58
Nonwhite	34	50	39	68	73	42

Note: Tumblr, Reddit, and WhatsApp not shown. Nonwhite includes all racial and ethnic groups, except non-Hispanic white.
Source: Survey conducted Aug. 8-21, 2017.
"News Use Across Social Media Platforms 2017"

PEW RESEARCH CENTER

Figure 3.2 Where do you get your news? If the answer is on Facebook, Instagram, or Snapchat, you're not alone.

So, where do our students get their news? We're betting that very few people who work with kids (who have access to mobile devices) will be surprised that the answer is Snapchat. Among the social media platforms studied by Pew, Snapchat attracted, by far, the youngest group of news users (Shearer & Gottfried, 2017). According to the same Pew study, 82% of Snapchat users who reported using the app for news consumption were between the ages of 18–29. As you can see in Figure 3.2, this was the youngest demographic group in the study. Snapchat, however, allows account holders as young as 13.

In addition, Snapchat conducted its own survey of account holders who use the app for news consumption. As you can see in Figure 3.3, the survey revealed that about half of Snapchat users who report following news media or journalists on the app see having a Snapchat account as helping that media outlets' or journalists' credibility. In other words, having a Snapchat account was viewed as a sort of endorsement. If Snapchat users can follow a reporter on the app, they are more likely to trust that journalist's or media outlet's

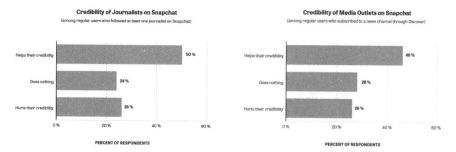

Figure 3.3 It's a snap! Being a Snapchat account holder boosts journalists' credibility with other Snapchat users.

news stories, compared to stories from a person or entity that does not have an account (Stroud & Gomez, 2017).

When we share this finding with educators at conferences or workshops, the responses are always the same: the adults in the room lament the poor information skills of young people and are shocked to learn that something as simple as being connected to a media outlet via Snapchat could be an influencing factor in determining credibility. But let's take a step back and think about this for a minute. Is this phenomenon really that surprising? And is it truly exclusive to younger, more naive information consumers? We don't think so, because it has happened to us, too.

From Honorary Gator to First-Name "Friend"

A few years back, Jennifer had an idea for a reading promotion at her middle school. Called "Gators Read Everywhere" (after the school mascot), the project involved collecting pins on a Google map to highlight photos of her students and teachers reading in various locations. She envisioned it being used not only to get kids excited about reading, but also as a tool for content-area instruction in math and social studies classes. Because she taught at a school with a mid-to-high poverty level, her dream of a map featuring pins from all over the world was soon dashed by the reality that her students (and teachers) simply didn't have the resources to snap photos of themselves reading very far beyond the borders of their school and neighborhoods.

As any connected educator might, Jennifer then took her problem to Twitter and asked her personal learning network (PLN) to contribute photos to expand the map's reach. One of the first people to respond to this request was author Neil Gaiman, who sent a photo of himself reading on a train near Cardiff, Wales. From there, other photos started to pour in, not just from her PLN, but also from authors who were inspired by Gaiman, and who were then connected with Jennifer's students, because they were all "honorary Gators" (Figure 3.4).

Library Girl @jenniferlagarde
Looking for help w/this project. Any honorary gators out there? http://bit.ly/cE4VGs #tlchat #edchat #engchat

Neil Gaiman Reads...
Last Updated by Jennifer LaGarde on Oct 21, 2010

HONORARY GATOR Neil Gaiman, Newbery and Carnegie Medal winner, author of *The Graveyard Book, Odd and the Frost Giants, Coraline*, (and many others), reads Italian Folktales by Italo Calvino...

- late at night.
- on a train.
- somewhere near Cardiff, Wales

Figure 3.4 When Neil Gaiman responds to your tweet, things get real.

What does this have to do with credibility and Snapchat? In the weeks following Neil Gaiman's reply and Retweet of her request, Jennifer felt more closely connected to the Newbery Award–winning author. Her brief, virtual, but direct, contact with him created the illusion that they were BFFs. For weeks after, she would refer to him as "Neil—we're on a first-name basis now—Gaiman." Like young news consumers more highly valuing journalists who hold Snapchat accounts, the shared social media connection influenced Jennifer's perception of her Twitter encounter. In this context, it's a little harder to shake our heads in dismay or waggle our fingers at young news consumers when considering the effect that being connected to journalists on Snapchat has on them. These connections, however small, give us the illusion that a relationship exists—and that's no accident.

Connections Influence Perception

Because social media requires users to *connect* with others in order to get the most out of the experience, we become invested in these tools in ways that we cannot with those that provide more passive media consumption, such as television and print journalism. Social media relies on us contributing and connecting with others who belong to our networks, and those connections only increase our desire to be part of what's happening on each site or app. The creators of these tools rely on these connections feeling personal. And when they do, they influence our actions both on and off screen.

So, no, it's not that surprising to hear Snapchat users report that they trust journalists who have Snapchat accounts more than those who do not. And if we're really honest about our own consumption of news through social media, we have to admit that these connections influence us, too.

Of course, this applies to people beyond news outlets and journalists as well. Most of us have carefully curated our networks to include, primarily friends, family, and professional contacts that we trust or admire. When those people in our networks share news stories, they have an advantage over other people with whom we are not connected: We already trust them. That trust leads us to assume that what they share has been vetted by them in some way. Unfortunately, that vetting doesn't always occur, which can lead to inadvertently spreading inaccurate information. When we Like, share, or otherwise engage with content that we believe to be reliable *only* because we hold the person sharing it in high esteem, we are potentially exacerbating the problem. This can be as innocuous as spreading a false report about a celebrity's untimely death, but it can also carry more serious consequences such as those that occurred when millions of people passed on the false story of Frida Sofia trapped in the earthquake rubble, which the Introduction discussed. Although mistakes may seem innocent enough, as educators we must assume that at least some of the folks who follow us trust that what we're posting is accurate without double-checking us, for the very same reasons. Before we know it, our social media feeds start to resemble the old shampoo commercial in which I tell two friends, and then they tell two friends, who tell two more friends, and so on and so forth until we can no longer discern what's real and what isn't amongst all that lather.

A Buffet of Options: Helping Students Choose?

We are living in exponential times—an era in which change is not only constant, but also so rapid that it can be difficult to keep up with. This is especially relevant to educators who, in the face of ever-changing expectations and available resources, continue to strive to prepare the students of today for the world of tomorrow. If there was a time when we could simply point our students to a curated list of credible resources and call it research, those days are over. Because the platforms by which we access news no longer represent definitive ways of determining credibility, the more we know about *how* young people consume news, the more we can help students improve at discerning fact from fiction.

Our students face an overwhelming assortment of options for getting their news. Their parents' and teachers' generations relied on a few traditional resources (newspapers, TV, and radio), and because those sources were vetted and edited by professional journalists, consumers could be reasonably assured of their reliability. However, as Bob Dylan sang, "The times, they are a-changin'" (1964). Today, news can, and does, come from anywhere in an ever-multiplying buffet of options. Blogs, social media, instant messages, texts, app alerts, YouTube, GIFs, emojis, and, of course, websites curated by both traditional and citizen journalists readily supplement or even replace those traditional formats. And how do students access all these sources? On their smartphones. And they aren't alone. According to 2016 research conducted by the John S. and James L. Knight foundation,

> since 2011, the rate of adult U.S. smartphone ownership has increased notably from 46 to 82 percent, and is nearing a saturation point among some age groups. In just the past two years, individual mobile news consumption has grown rapidly. In fact, 89 percent of the U.S. mobile population (144 million users) now access news and information via mobile devices. (Knight, 2016)

Although no surprise, the fact that the younger generation uses their phones for news consumption does matter insomuch as it should cause educators to consider how often they create research opportunities for students to use these very devices. We're not suggesting that teachers abandon their laptops or tablets when creating instructional opportunities for young people, but we do advocate that we allow our kids to also use the devices in their pockets. After all, if smartphones are the tools students are using outside of school to access news, then shouldn't they be able to use the same tools at school too—at least sometimes?

What Is a Primary Source?

In a later report by the Knight Foundation, titled "How Youth Navigate the News Landscape," researchers further explored the way young people consumed news on mobile and social media (Madden, Lenhart, & Fontaine, 2017). Some trends they identified should also give us pause as we consider our role in helping students become effective news consumers. For example, young people have an evolving opinion of what constitutes "news" that reinterprets the traditional term *primary source* for the digital era to include user-generated content that is streamed on YouTube and similar sites. In later chapters, we'll dig a little deeper into how news looks different when accessed on mobile devices, but for now consider:

- How many of your research assignments allow for the citation of YouTube videos, blogs, or Instagram posts as acceptable sources of information?
- Do you include such digital documents when teaching students about primary sources?
- How do your students interact with and contribute to the information found on such sources?
- How do these online sources stack up next to more traditional news sources in helping your students (and you) make sense of the world?

The answers to these questions matter less than the process of asking them and then using the answers to guide instructional decision-making. As the saying goes, "It's okay to be where you are. It's just not okay to stay there."

Often employed as a cautionary tale to warn young people about the dangers of posting (potentially) incriminating information about themselves online, the story of the Georgia teenager whose Snapchat selfie with a murder victim became a key piece of evidence in his subsequent murder trial also provides a valuable, if macabre, lesson for educators (Cook, 2015). If the criminal justice system views social media posts as reliable pieces of evidence to identify and convict criminals, surely we need to rethink our use of them as primary sources. No longer can we restrict that label to bloodstained journals found on the battlefield. We must broaden our view of what constitutes an acceptable source of information to capture those already trusted by our students. At the same time and of equal importance, we must also identify new ways of defining source credibility so that the research skills we teach in school transfer to the often higher stakes research and information consumption our learners conduct when we're not there to guide them.

News by Notification

Knight researchers also found that rather than actively *seeking* the news, the teens they interviewed *discovered* news by setting up notifications on their phones or by following newsmakers on social media (Madden, Lenhart, & Fontaine, 2017). In this way, the news came to them, rather than the other way around. Many educators teach their students to find credible information sources, but how many teach students how to set up their own algorithms for ensuring those same credible sources come to them? In other words, to what extent does your media literacy program include the creation of reliable and unbiased notification systems? Rather than asking our learners to conform to how *we* seek out news, our media literacy efforts should, to some degree, conform to how *students* prefer to receive information in the context of their life outside of school.

A Call to Accuracy

In 2016, *Rolling Stone* journalist Tim Dickinson Tweeted about the pervasive use of the term *fake news*. We agree with Dickinson's call for precision, which is shown in Figure 3.5. When we use the term *fake news*, we over simplify what is often a carefully crafted attempt to

Figure 3.5 Follow Tim Dickinson's lead: Don't use "lazy language," identify the true problem. Posted by user @7im Tim Dickinson about "fake news" shortly after the 2016 U.S. Presidential Election.

influence opinion using a variety of strategies. Let's unpack those that Dickenson identifies:

- ᛦ **Propaganda:** "Ideas, facts, or allegations spread deliberately to further one's cause or to damage an opposing cause" (Merriam-Webster, 2018). We often associate propaganda with something that is created by an official office or government entity to further its own agenda.

- ᛦ **Disinformation:** "False information deliberately and often covertly spread (as by the planting of rumors) in order to influence public opinion or obscure the truth" (Merriam-Webster, 2018). Although similar to propaganda, disinformation differs in that it is often spread to discredit a rival rather than promote one's own agenda.

- ᛦ **Conspiracy Theory:** "A theory that explains an event or set of circumstances as the result of a secret plot by usually powerful conspirators" (Merriam-Webster, 2018). Conspiracy theories are typically spread as part of a disinformation campaign to discredit a rival.

- ᛦ **Clickbait:** "Something (such as a headline) designed to make readers want to click on a hyperlink especially when the link leads to content of dubious value or interest" (Merriam-Webster, 2018). These sensational headlines often make claims that are either completely unrelated to or are not proved by the information in the article. The dramatic headlines, however, entice people to click and, even more desirable on the part of the site's creators and advertisers, to share the article, repeating whatever outrageous claim is contained in the title.

To these we would add a couple of more options:

- ᛦ **Satire:** "A way of using humor to show that someone or something is foolish, weak, bad, etc.; humor that shows the weaknesses or bad qualities of a person, government, society, etc." (Merriam-Webster, 2018). Online satire publications, such as

The Onion (theonion.com) and *The Borowitz Report* (from *The New Yorker*), publish intentionally false and outlandish news stories for comedic purposes. In 2017, *The Washington Post* reported that Chinese media had picked up one of these intentionally false news stories (claiming that President Trump had ordered all White House telephones be covered in tin foil) and published it as true. Unfortunately, this isn't an isolated incident.

- **Bias Challenging**: Anything that doesn't confirm our own biases. More and more, people (both in and out of the public eye) have begun using the term *fake news* to discredit anything that challenges their existing beliefs. "If it doesn't confirm what I already believe," their flawed reasoning goes, "it must be fake."

These distinctions become especially important when we consider how best to teach students to spot suspect news stories. The reality is that suspect stories of all types are being created, at an exponential rate, by an entire industry that exists solely to influence and fool information consumers (Dickinson, 2016).

Exposing a new industry in Eastern Europe that only continues to grow, NBC News profiled an anonymous web content creator called Dimitri, who identified himself as just one of many young people living in Vales, Macedonia, who earned a relative king's salary from creating false news stories, featuring clickbait headlines and disinformation, for social media targeting Americans prior to the 2016 U.S. presidential election. According to the NBC's December, 2016, report, the articles Dimitri and his colleagues created were "sensationalist and often baseless, [but] were posted to Facebook, drawing in armies of readers and earning fake-news writers money from penny-per-click advertising." Dimitri stated he earned over $60,000 in six months, which in a community where the average annual wage is just $4,800 made the teenager one of the richest men in town. The report went on to describe how Dimitri and fellow fake news entrepreneurs had changed the economy of the town, citing the influx of their incomes saving businesses and creating new cottage industries to cater to the new class of young, wealthy people like Dimitri. In the last minutes of the interview, he says that if fake news affected the outcome of the U.S. election, it's not his fault. Rather, Dimitri laid blame squarely at the feet of "foolish" Americans and stated that citizens in other parts of the world take democracy more seriously, and that they would never "fall for such hoax news stories" (Smith and Banic, 2016).

Whether or not you agree with Dimitri's choice of career, he is right about at least one thing: The onus is on the consumers of news to make sure that we base our opinions and actions on facts. Dimitri's story is also an incredibly useful instructional tool. Too often, our discussions about *why* students should care about media literacy revolve around citations and the consequence of poor grades if they cite an incorrect source. That said, if the threat of academic reprisal does motivate kids at all, that motivation is temporary, evaporating once the assignment is complete. Our students are capable of, and deserve, more meaningful discussions that include the reality of what we're facing as news consumers. Applying healthy skepticism to all the information we read is about more than jumping through a few hoops in order to comply with a teacher's expectations. Rather, it's about defying the expectations of people like Dimitri who expect us to fall for his cleverly crafted attempts to fool us. As the great American philosopher Obi-Wan Kenobi once said, "Who is more foolish, the fool or the fool who follows him?" (1977). Our students won't want to be a fool of either type.

In the NBC report and the countless others like it, Dimitri and other content creators share their strategies for writing stories that are more likely to fool information consumers and result in more clicks and shares, which Google AdSense revenue schemes rely on. Their writing strategies mirror the descriptors Tim Dickinson encourages us to use in place of the "lazy" term *fake news*. In addition, they rely on *confirmation bias*, which is the tendency to interpret new evidence as confirmation of one's existing beliefs or theories (Casad, 2016).

According to CNN, the fake news industry in Macedonia is "gearing up" for the 2020 U.S. election, so the flood of fabrications isn't a problem that is going away anytime soon (Soares, 2017). One tool to help students navigate it safely is the infographic shown in Figure 3.6 and created by the European Association for Viewers Interests (EAVI), a nonprofit organization focused on "empowering individuals to be active, engaged citizens in today's increasingly challenging media environment" (Steinberg, 2017).

Figure 3.6 As fake news creators prepare for future elections, resources like this, and those shared in Chapter 6, help students quickly identify suspect information sources.

This tool helps students (and teachers) dissect suspect news stories to determine whether or not they are trustworthy by digging deeper than simply defining the information as real of fake.

Fake News Fatigue

One other consequence of getting more and more of our news on our mobile devices is that it's difficult to escape from both the news itself and the constant shouting about whether or not a news story can be trusted. One of the students interviewed for the Knight Foundation study shared her habit of checking her phone first thing in the morning, seeing the news alerts that had collected overnight, and feeling a certain amount of anxiety as a result (Madden, Lenhart, & Fontaine, 2017). Not only can we relate, but we're betting you can too! Additionally, this nonstop information barrage leads to a sort of "fake news fatigue." It's tempting to just throw up our hands and surrender to the perceived reality that this is just the world we live in and now: Everything is fake and nothing is true, so why even bother? *The New York Times* captured this same sentiment in its article "As Fake News Spreads, More Readers Shrug at Truth" stating, "Fake news, and the proliferation of raw opinion that passes for news, is creating confusion, punching holes in what is true, causing a kind of fun-house effect that leaves the reader doubting everything, including real news" (Tavernise, 2016). Our students are, of course, not immune to this fatigue. In fact, it may account for some of the apathy that educators report when trying to get kids interested in source credibility. We believe that one way to avoid this fatigue is to focus on language that helps our learners unpack what's really going on, which is where infographics such as Figure 3.5 can help. By being more specific about the ways a news story can be biased or false, we provide students with greater tools for spotting fake news, while also avoiding the overuse of a phrase that can cause us all to tune out.

Implications for Schools

Obviously, all the issues we've discussed in this chapter have far-reaching implications for schools. As part of our research for *Fact vs. Fiction*, we shared a brief online survey with our PLNs via social media about if and how members were addressing the issue of fake news with the students they serve. Although 87% of respondents said they taught media literacy in some way, only 7% said that their school or district had identified any instructional goals for helping students navigate fake news. Even fewer (6.5%) said that their district had invested in or identified a media literacy curriculum for educators to use, while the other 93.5% said they'd created their own

(LaGarde & Hudgins, 2018). (Many of the resources these educators identified as being part of what they used to help their learners build capacity as information consumers will be discussed in later chapters.) The sentiments expressed by those who responded to our survey overwhelmingly reflected the feedback we received when working with educators in their districts or during conference workshops:

- ♀ Our students (and many of our teachers) need quality media literacy instruction now more than ever.
- ♀ The effectiveness of attempts to implement such instruction can be hindered by a lack of district and/or school policies related to internet filtering and student access to devices.

A Different Kind of Filter Bubble

All school districts have to block student access to inappropriate websites in order to be compliant with the Children's Internet Protection Act (CIPA). And, we can all agree that students don't need to be accessing the kind of content CIPA was designed to protect them from (pornography, extreme violence, and the like). In our experience, however, many districts use internet filtering as a form of classroom management or as a means of saving bandwidth. Unfortunately, the software installed by district technology departments often blocks websites with legitimate educational purposes, as well as such social networking sites such as Facebook, Twitter, YouTube, Instagram, and Snapchat. Even when students bring their own devices to school or try to connect to a guest Wi-Fi via their mobile devices, access to these sites is frequently blocked. What's more, teachers frequently have to jump through numerous hoops to request that the sites be unblocked, and even then, there's no guarantee that those requests will be successful. The American Library Association addresses the conflict between all-too-common filtering practices and critical instructional goals in its statement for Banned Website Week:

> Filtering websites does the next generation of digital citizens a disservice. Students must develop skills to evaluate information from all types of sources in multiple formats, *including the Internet*. Relying solely on filters does not teach young citizens how to be savvy searchers or how to evaluate the accuracy of information. (2011)

Although we all agree that some content must be filtered in order to ensure our students remain safe online, decisions about which websites need to be blocked should be rooted in a desire to make school more relevant to students and enhance their learning experiences. This is especially true as it relates to media and information literacy. As we've already established, the ways in which our students access news are different from generations before them. Policies set at the district level that affect how they access that same information at school should be informed by what the research says about our learners as news consumers, rather than being based on what makes life easier for adults.

Equity, Access, and Citizenship

Of course, when we talk about access as it pertains to digital resources and how they can be used to build student capacity as creators and consumers, we're not just talking about filtering. Research conducted by Mark Warschauer at the University of California, Irvine revealed some troubling truths regarding how school-district technology resources are used among students of different races and income levels. Warschauer found that "overall, students who are Black, Hispanic, or low-income are more likely to use computers for drill-and-practice, whereas students who are White or high-income are more likely to use computers for simulations or authentic applications" (Zielezinski, 2016). This is troubling on a number of levels, but it is especially distressing when we consider the potential impact of denying marginalized students access to tools and resources (or opportunities to use them in meaningful ways) that are so deeply tied to what it means to be a citizen today. Put another way, tools such as Facebook, YouTube, and Snapchat are more than just social media, search engines, or even news sources; they are also the tools of our democracy. In addition to being places where students learn about what is happening in the world, they are also communities where they (and we) can interact with our elected officials.

When the students of Marjory Stoneman Douglas High School in Parkland, Florida, wanted to create awareness around the issue of school violence and gun control, they did not write letters to their senators or create phone banks to bombard their congress people with phone calls. Rather, they started a massive online movement using social media that has affected campaigns and how advertisers choose to support media personalities who have been critical of their efforts (Newcomb, 2018). Whether we agree with these teenagers or not, it's difficult not to marvel at how effective they have been at harnessing tools—tools that are largely blocked in school—to create changes that could deeply affect everyone in those buildings. In the context of this example, it becomes clear that situations in which some students are given the opportunity to use tools in ways that build this capacity while others are not is untenable. When we deny poor or minority students access to the tools of our democracy, we are failing to prepare them to participate in their government.

Whose Responsibility Is It?

One of the questions we frequently get when working with educators on how to address fake news with students has to do with whose responsibility it is to teach this stuff in the first place. The quick answer, of course, is everyone! We believe media literacy is best taught in context, so that students can see how the principles of source credibility, identifying bias, and so on apply to all disciplines, and are not just something that has to be done in a specific class.

As we mentioned in Chapter 2, according to the Center on Education Policy, which has examined the impact of No Child Left Behind (NCLB) on curriculum, the time that students at all grade levels spend in history or civics courses has been greatly reduced in the last decade. This matters insomuch as history and social studies courses have traditionally been places for students to explore such topics as current events, the role of the press and the historical context of propaganda. Today's students are exposed to exponentially more information than any other generation of learners before them, and yet, they are provided less time in the courses in which the curricula is best matched to help them navigate their complex world.

Similarly, according to the National Center of Education Statistics (NCES), between 2000 and 2016 schools lost the equivalent of more than 10,000 full-time school librarian positions, or about 19% of the total school librarian workforce, nationwide (Lance, 2018). Despite numerous statewide, longitudinal studies providing a wealth of evidence that children and adolescents benefit when they attend schools with degreed librarians (Lance, 2014), continued cuts to these positions mean that fewer students have access to the one person in the school whose training focuses, in part, on media literacy and source evaluation. Additionally, because school librarians teach every child, work with every teacher, and understand the curricula at all grade levels, they are well positioned to support classroom teachers as they take on the challenge of helping students become expert navigators of the news and information landscape.

Without these key positions and instructional time allotted to content that addresses desperately needed media literacy skills, our students are put at a disadvantage. Further, you'll see in the chapters to follow how school librarians are on the front lines of combatting the effects of fake news on our students. What's more, because these reductions in positions and instructional time have not proven to be the silver bullet solution to low test scores (Straus, 2015), it's time for school districts to start prioritizing learning over testing, by reinvesting in the school librarians and content curricula, both of which are proven to prepare students for more than just the multiple-choice assessment at the end of the year.

Great Challenges Require Great Solutions

Although this point in history may well be one of the most exciting times ever to be an educator, it also represents a point in time when it is both exceedingly challenging and critically important that we help our students navigate the information world they are inheriting from us. As you've seen in this chapter, the ways in which we get our news and the realities of how other people in the world have found great wealth in exploiting them, alongside cuts to the very positions and instructional opportunities that are best able to prepare our kids for this reality, all equate to what seems like a perfect storm. And while we're optimistic about our chances, we also feel a great sense of urgency around these issues. We have the ability to right the ship. What we need is the will. We must prioritize resources and create budgets that reflect our values. As we'll see in the next chapter, the consequences of not doing so are dire.

Chapter 3

1. Consider the last photo you posted. Did you use Facetune to take away a few wrinkles? Apply a filter to set the mood? We are all creating and altering digital age primary sources all the time. How can we change existing research projects to help sharpen our students' skills in discerning whether or not online content has been altered and what the purpose of those alterations might be?

2. Rate your own familiarity with the tools your students use regularly to access news and information. What implications does your answer have on your own professional learning?

Not at all familiar ●———●———●———●———● Very familiar

3. Tweet us! What are some ways your school or district is working to make sure *all* students have equitable access to technology that includes opportunities for them to grow as information consumers and creators?

Our Brains on Fake News

By the time you have reached adulthood, your brain has decided how the world works—how a table looks and feels, how liquids and authority figures behave, how scary are rats. It has made countless billions of little insights and decisions. It has made its mind up. From then on in, its treatment of any new information that runs counter to those views can sometimes be brutal. Your brain is surprisingly reluctant to change its mind. Rather than going through the difficulties involved in rearranging itself to reflect the truth, it often prefers to fool you. So it distorts. It forgets. It projects. It lies.

—Will Storr, *The Unpersuadables: Adventures with the Enemies of Science*

In December of 2017, a North Carolina man walked into a Washington, D.C. pizza parlor to "self investigate" an online conspiracy theory known as "Pizzagate" that suggested the restaurant was harboring a child sex-trafficking ring with connections to former presidential candidate Hillary Clinton. Investigated by the local police department and the FBI, these claims had been declared false. Still, armed with the information he'd read and watched online, an AR-15 assault rifle, a .38 handgun, and a folding knife, he entered the crowded restaurant and began shooting, opening doors, and looking for the basement where the children were supposedly being held captive. He did not find any captive children. Nor did he find a basement, because the restaurant did not have one. What he did find was a quick response by the police who apprehended him before anyone was hurt. He was later sentenced to four years in prison (Robb, 2017).

In January of 2016, a Florida woman began sending emails to and leaving threatening voicemails for the father of Noah Pozner, a 6-year-old boy who was among the twenty children and six adults shot and killed by gunman Adam Lanza at Sandy Hook Elementary School in Newtown, Connecticut, in December 2012. The woman was driven to send Pozner messages threatening his life because she believed the Sandy Hook tragedy was a hoax: an incident fabricated by liberals in conspiracy with government officials to build support for gun control legislation. As *The Washington Post* reported when the perpetrator of these threats was sentenced to four years in prison, "Sandy Hook hoaxers have peddled conspiracy theories about the mass shooting in online message boards, blogs and grainy YouTube videos. There is no credible evidence supporting these claims" (Hawkins, 2017). And yet the claims, along with countless others, flourished in a new "post-truth" information ecosystem: a space where false claims are defended as absolute facts.

In November 2017, CNN International published a story exposing a human trafficking ring in Libya. Footage obtained by an undercover journalist captured a slave auction in which men being held captive were sold to bidders gathered in Tripoli for as little as $400 American dollars. The story sparked international outrage, and the footage, along with other evidence collected by CNN, was turned over to the Libyan government after it promised to launch an investigation. A few weeks later, however, the Libyan government called the credibility of the evidence into question citing Tweets from U.S. President Trump, in which he accused CNN of spreading "fake news." A Libyan broadcaster echoed the government's suspicion of CNN stating, "Here the possibility arises that the channel has published the report of slavery in Libya to secure an as yet hidden political objective." Citing the U.S. president's Tweets, the Libyan government then announced that an internal investigation of the human trafficking story would be preceded instead by an investigation of CNN (Wintour, 2017). To date, none of the information contained in CNN's original report has been proven false.

Fake Facts, Real Consequences

Incidents like these are a clear and chilling reminder that the propagation of false stories and the labeling of legitimate journalism as fake have real consequences to us as human beings. Although actual violence and death threats may be relatively rare, more and more Americans are reporting harassment as a result of online activity. The 2017 Pew Research Center's Online Harassment Report indicated that four in ten U.S. adults have personally experienced harassing or abusive behavior online and 18% have been the target of severe behaviors, such as physical threats or sexual harassment (Duggan, 2017). There's nothing fake about the impact of fake news on our daily lives and on those of our students.

Rising Discord

A December 2016 article in *School Library Journal* titled "Hate Incidents in Libraries Spark a Renewed Commitment to Serve All" described an "increase in harassment and hate speech against people of color, immigrants, and LGBTQ students" since the 2016 presidential election (Cottrell, 2016). The article featured stories from around the country in which librarians recounted incidents of library books being defaced with swastikas or public spaces tagged with racist graffiti. Perhaps most troubling were the stories in which students of color and of religious minorities shared their fears of being targeted and that they felt frightened of their classmates. Libraries—spaces that have always been symbols of open discourse—were suddenly on the front lines of a culture war where information and its reliability were front and center.

Just one month earlier, the Southern Poverty Law Center (SPLC) conducted a survey of more than 10,000 teachers, counselors, administrators, and other educators to determine what, if any, effect the 2016 U.S. presidential election had had on schools and students. According to the SPLC's findings, "90% of educators report that school climate has been negatively affected, and most of them believe it will have a long-lasting impact. A full 80% describe heightened anxiety and concern on the part of students worried about the impact of the election on themselves and their families" (Lindberg, 2016). Regardless of your opinions of the outcome of the presidential election, the anecdotes recounted in the survey, ranging from vandalism to physical attacks, are very difficult to read. But one thing they share is the repetition of phrases that the students surveyed had heard at home or in the media in the lead up to the election. The frequency and ease of which the phrases, including racial, religious, or other epithets, were heard by adults seemed to embolden their use by students at school.

A Tale of Two Walls

In 2016, Nikki D Robertson was working as a school librarian in a bustling high school near Huntsville, Alabama. As is often the case in large schools, the library served multiple roles and was also the location where daily ELL (English language learner) classes were held. To give students a place to post positive messages, share poetry or artwork, and the like, Nikki transformed one large windowed wall into a Student Voice Wall. Shortly after the U.S. presidential election, however, Nikki arrived at school to find that one of her students had written "Build that wall!" on the glass right where the ELL students (many of whom were from Mexico or other Spanish speaking countries) could see it (Figure 4.1). Devastated, Nikki immediately followed up to find out who had defaced the library, and (perhaps unknowingly) harassed these students, by tagging the space with a phrase that had been used often and divisively at campaign events and in election news in relation to preventing immigrants entering the U.S.

Figure 4.1 Divisive slogans on a high school's Student Voice Wall are an attack on empathy.

Taking the student aside, she asked him to consider how his ELL classmates might have felt when they heard the phrase on TV or the radio, only to then also see it written by another student at school. She then reminded him that since the Student Voice Wall had been created, political statements had never been allowed, because she did not want the space to become divisive. Contrite, the student erased what he'd written and apologized. But the next day, someone else had written the same thing.

Soon, many of the ELL students came to Nikki to report that they were in fear of their classmates, and that their families might be deported. "I remember holding kids' hands as they shook and cried. These kids were in tatters," Nikki said recounting the event later when interviewed for this book. As with many of the educators who responded to the SPLC survey, Nikki responded that she did not feel supported by her administration, which didn't want to become embroiled in a political debate at the expense of focusing on academics. In the end, Nikki ended up removing the wall as a place for students to write, because what had once been a visual representation of the idea that all voices were valued in the library had been turned into something far darker. What was perhaps an already existing chasm of understanding between these two groups of students grew impassable as a result, and left Nikki questioning her decision to work in public education (Robertson, personal communication, June 11, 2018).

When we take a close, hard look at all of these stories in combination, a glaring truth stares back at us: Fake news affects our ability to empathize with others and to consider that points of views that contradict our own might also be valid. This attack on empathy is at the heart of what makes fake news so insidious and, as such, must also be at the heart of how we approach media literacy with our students.

Fake News Strategies, Bias, and Empathy

As we've discussed previously, purveyors of false news stories use a variety of strategies for helping their work spread and saturate:

- They rely on clickbait titles, often featuring famous or familiar names and places to pique our interest.
- They bombard us with brief, repeated versions of the same story.
- They often include at least some facts to make it difficult to pick out what is real and what is fake.

- ♀ They model their articles, videos, and other media so that they are almost indistinguishable from legitimate news counterparts.
- ♀ They include (sometimes completely fabricated or taken out of context) "eyewitness" testimonials to add legitimacy.
- ♀ They rely on fear and propaganda to inflame existing anxieties.
- ♀ They take advantage of our tendency to trust information that confirms our existing biases, which also increases the likelihood of an emotional investment on the reader's part.

These strategies are important because they also take advantage of natural weaknesses in the human brain. "Through networks such as Twitter and Facebook, users are exposed daily to a large number of transmissible pieces of information that compete to attain success," wrote the authors of a recent study in the journal *Nature and Human Behaviour*. The authors went on to say that "discriminating between good and bad information has become more important in today's online information networks than ever before." And yet, even though the stakes are higher, the brain's ability to distinguish real from fake under the constant barrage of new information is diminished. And, when faced with an information onslaught, most people end up privileging popularity over credibility (Qiu, Oliveira, Shirazi, Flammini, & Menczer, 2017). Not only is this a deadly combination for information overload and our brain's inability to cope with such rapid-fire information, but also the nonstop repetition of negative messaging that plays off our fears and biases begins to take root, replacing empathy for other people with fear and resentment.

And this has real consequences for those of us working in education. Thom Markham, an educator, consultant, and project-based learning (PBL) expert, wrote in a 2016 article for *Mindshift* that "empathy lies at the heart of 21st century skillfulness in teamwork, collaboration, and communication in a diverse world." He went on to explain how having empathy for others, that is to say, the ability to compare one's own experiences and ideas to someone else's and to have that comparison result in the feeling of being able to understand or share them, triggers creativity, enables us to collaborate with people whose experiences differ from our own, and helps us to solve complex problems that might challenge our existing beliefs. According to Markham, "empathy has the potential to open up students to deeper learning, drive clarity of thinking, and inspire engagement with the world—in other words, provide the emotional sustenance for outstanding human performance" (Markham, 2016).

In this way, the fake news phenomenon should cause us concern for more than just our students' ability to determine if a source is reliable. We should also be on the lookout for signs that it is eroding a fundamental element of what binds us together as people. Consider these two facts: First, in 2016, nearly a million people viewed, Liked, and shared a completely fake news story on Facebook claiming that newly elected U.S. President Trump executed five Thanksgiving turkeys pardoned the year before by President Obama (Silverman, 2017). Second, in that same year, teachers in an elementary school in Minnesota reported that after a few White, male students were caught grabbing the genitals of their female, Hispanic classmates, the boys explained that they hadn't done anything wrong because such actions had become legal after the election (Lindberg, 2016). At first blush, it may seem as though these two events are unrelated, but they are inextricably linked. Even if we know, objectively, that a news story is false, biased, or, in the case of the turkeys, just plain silly, the constant repetition of information that pits us against one another erodes our ability to empathize with people who are different from us. Our students are listening to the same stories being repeated on television and on the radio as we are. They see the same headlines we do on social media. This constant repetition in the form of sensational and biased headlines or sound bites takes root in their brains, just as it does in ours, creating a new standard for acceptable behavior. It also emboldens those with deeply held biases to express them in far more public and aggressive ways.

In the Southern Poverty Law Center study, a smaller, but still important group of educators reported that although their students were affected by the language used by adults and the media in the lead up to the 2016 U.S. presidential election, those impacts did *not* translate to hostile actions on campus. The study's authors described their schools as "schools that have worked hard at establishing inclusive welcoming communities, have response programs in place, and nurtured qualities of empathy and compassion among students" (Lindberg, 2016). This proves that if we're going to combat fake news and its effects on our campuses, we must focus on more than just evaluating sources and all that it entails in the digital age. We also must start seeing empathy as a wellness barometer, one that helps us determine whether our students are cognitively ready to tackle the hard work of determining what's real, what isn't, what's been created to deceive us, and what might challenge our existing and deeply held points of view. We then can employ approaches to media literacy that also strengthen this fundamental quality.

Strengthening Your Core (Principles)

While we can't provide you with a replicable set of sure-fire lesson plans that are guaranteed to shatter your students' biases while simultaneously sharpening their information skills, we *can* provide you with Five Core Principles to apply as you create lessons and units that are tailored to your individual students:

1. Be aware of your own biases.
2. Think about technology as tools for building empathy.
3. Arm students with language that allows them to challenge ideas, but that does not attack people.
4. Model positive behavior in your own digital and analog interactions.
5. Give students the chance to reflect.

Let's take a closer look at each principle.

Be Aware of Your Own Biases

As human beings, we all want to be correct. We all want to do what is right. What's more, we look for messages in the world that support those desires, while finding it easy to dismiss those that don't. If we're going to help our students accept these tendencies in themselves (and the other adults in their lives) we must first accept it in ourselves. So too, should we share examples of how those biases led us to be fooled by false information. There's no shame in being fooled. The shame is in failing to learn from it.

Think About Technology as Tools for Building Empathy

When it comes to media literacy, we often think of technology as just tools for locating, curating, and sharing information, but there are lots of ways to use the devices your students already have to help build empathy. Some ways to do this are:

- Provide kids with the opportunity to give and receive authentic feedback from their peers and, when appropriate, learners and experts beyond the four walls of the school. Whether you use Google Classroom (classroom.google.com/h), digital portfolios on Seesaw (web.seesaw.me), a class blog, or social media, kids need practice developing the skills of giving positive, productive feedback, while also experiencing how feedback to their own work makes them feel. These experiences can help them better navigate the treacherous comments sections beneath many information sources.

- Use technology to connect kids with learners and leaders from around the globe. Whether you use Skype (skype.com), YouTube Live (youtube.com/live), or some other streaming tool, the more opportunities we give learners to connect with real people whose experiences may be different from theirs, the more likely they are to realize that as humans we have more in common than we have differences. This fundamental truth is a powerful antidote to the stereotypes that are inherent in many fake news stories.

- Harness the power of augmented reality (AR) and virtual reality (VR) to provide all learners with the opportunity to look at the world through someone else's eyes. True empathy comes from the ability to compare our own experiences to those of others and find value in both. Being able to disagree with someone but still appreciate and acknowledge his or her humanity is a skill that must be developed. Tools like Google Expeditions (edu.google.com/expeditions) and DiscoveryVR (discoveryvr.com) can be used to help students explore areas of the world that are in the news or to allow them the chance to walk through the experiences of specific groups of people. Coupled with meaningful conversations that compare what they've seen with related news stories or what they previously believed to be true about these people and places, AR and VR can help students consider how some sources of information fail to tell the whole story.

Arm Students with Language That Allows Them to Challenge Ideas, Not Attack People

Looking at sources of information, especially in the context of current events, can result in language or behavior that triggers anxiety for some students. It's important to create a set of norms for your classroom that define what is acceptable and what is not. We recommend that these guidelines be specific and that students play an integral role in creating these norms for the learning space they share with you. It's okay to encourage kids to generically "be kind," but only if that is followed up with real examples of what kindness looks like. Similarly, it's important to teach kids how to separate people from ideas. We might disagree with someone's ideas, and we can express that in any number of productive ways. Table 4.1 offers are some examples.

However you phrase it, we can't allow those conversations to devolve into insults or aggressive behavior. When we arm kids with specific language to help them navigate healthy debate, we are also giving them tools to recognize when news stories are rooted in personal attacks rather than in objective facts about an issue, policy, or event.

Model Positive Behavior in Your Own Digital and Analog Interactions

We often tell students that, no matter how secure our online accounts and social media feeds are, everything we post to the internet should be considered permanent and public. The same holds true for us. Even if your students are not following you on Instagram, subscribing to your YouTube channel, or hinging on all 240 characters of your every Tweet, there's a good chance some of their parents are—or someone who knows their parents or the other

Table 4.1 Ways to Challenge an Idea Without Diminishing a Person

Replace This Language ...	With ...
You are wrong.	I've seen some evidence that contradicts what you're saying, let me share it with you ...
I don't believe you.	Can you show me some research that helped you form that opinion? I'd like to learn more.
All people who believe that are _____.	We may not agree on this issue, but that doesn't mean we can't still be friends.
If you believe _____, then you're not a real _____.	I respect your right to disagree with me.

adults in their lives. If we expect our students (and colleagues) to vet sources of information before sharing them and exhibit empathy and good citizenship when interacting with others online, we need to do the same ourselves.

Give Students the Chance to Reflect

We cannot emphasize this enough. It is often said that "we do not learn from experience. We learn from reflecting on experience." Too often in school, reflection is relegated to a punishment for students who need to "learn from their behavior," when in fact all of our students need the opportunity to reflect on the experiences they've had in (and out) of our classrooms in order to truly make meaning from them. As you provide students with occasions to identify suspect news stories from those based in fact, and to develop empathy as part of the process of sharpening those skills, it's critical to also provide time and space for them to reflect on that learning. Whether it's a digital exit ticket, old-school journaling, or any number of other reflection strategies, don't forget to include this important step as part of your media literacy plan.

There Will Still Be Trolls

And yet, here is the truth of the matter: Even if we do all of this. Even if we have the best of intentions. Even if we plan and prepare and practice. There will still be "trolls." There will still be people with whom we cannot find common ground. There will still be those people who will hold firm to beliefs that we know are empirically false. Still. It is inevitable. In his book *The Unpersuadables: Adventures with Enemies of Science*, Will Storr sums up the feeling we get when digging into a position despite the existence of conflicting evidence: "Haven't we all done this? Hardened a particular position, not as a response to superior information, but because of anger?" (Storr, 2015).

Yes. Yes, we have.

By acknowledging this, we can help our students (and ourselves) better deal with situations wherein we confront people whose beliefs are immovable, despite mountains of conflicting, and empirically correct, evidence. Above the Noise, (a product of PBS Studios and KQED) created a great video for middle and high school students exploring the nature versus nurture argument as it relates to online trolls. The video not only helps students understand the difference between trolling and cyberbullying, but it also uses recent research to explain that although some trolls act out because of personality flaws, many are just seizing on an opportunity to get attention. In the anonymous context of the internet, it's easy to stir the pot with zero remorse, because rarely are there actual consequences for that behavior. Most of all, the video helps viewers see how easy it is to slip into that behavior given the right set of circumstances. It's all presented in a clear, easy-to-understand format that most students will respond to (2018).

That said, we feel trolling is related to our larger discussion about fake news in a couple of important ways. First, recent studies have shown that comments can actually influence the perceptions and opinions of otherwise objective readers. In other words, the more trolls leave negative comments about the stories being shared on a website, the more visitors to that site are likely to view the information being shared there as suspect (Daum, 2013). This further supports the fact that the brain tends to assimilate to the most popular or most frequently repeated opinion, regardless of its accuracy, when bombarded with information. Second, the way such credible news sources as NPR and *Popular Science* are dealing with trolls is interesting, too. Rather than expend resources on trying to monitor or change their behavior, organizations like these have simply eliminated spaces for public comments on their sites, choosing instead to invest in their social media presences (Green, 2017). This is consistent with the sage advice that has been handed down from one generation to the next since the time when the word *troll* conjured up images of scary monsters living under bridges: Don't feed them. The number one goal of trolls is to get attention. The more they get, the more they want. It's a vicious cycle. If we stop feeding them, they are more likely to just go away.

Don't Feed Fake News, Either

The same advice applies to fake news as well. The more we click on stories that are misleading, biased, or entirely false, the more these very same types of "new articles" will multiply. Fake news creators will give us more of whatever gets the most clicks. Whenever we click on and share a story that is suspect, we are providing Dimitri (see Chapter 3) and his fellow news creators with information about what we want to read. Just as we should stop feeding trolls, so too must we stop feeding Dimitris (Smith & Banic, 2016).

That said, how do we know if a news story is real or fake without clicking on it? Well, that is an excellent question and one we'd like to cheekily answer with a quote. As with all great quotes on the internet, to whom we should rightfully attribute the statement "The only thing necessary for evil to triumph is for good [people] to do nothing" (2018) is the subject of much debate. But whether it was Edward Burke or John F. Kennedy, we believe that when it comes to fake news, doing nothing (in this case, not clicking) is the most preferable response. Moreover, there are some strategies we can employ and teach our students to help everyone make reasonable judgments about a source's reliability without ever visiting the site. We'll discuss those in the next chapter, where we'll also give you the chance to put those strategies to the test.

Chapter 4

1. Educator Chad C. Everett posits that the end point of empathy is not feelings, but action. In other words, it's not enough to just *understand* how someone feels, we must *act* on that understanding. How can we use technology to help our students take actions that reflect their understanding of how others feel?

2. Which of the Five Core Principles shared in this chapter are the most challenging for you personally? What steps can you take to strengthen this area?

3. Tweet us! How is your school or district approaching incidents like those described in this chapter when political discord has affected behavior at school? Can you share some strategies for having these important, but sometimes sensitive, conversations with students? Colleagues? Parents?

CHAPTER 5

Fake News Self-Assessment

What might Albert Einstein—or Mark Twain—think about how technology, and the internet specifically, have affected how we access and evaluate information? (See Figure 5.1.) It's easy to imagine their disappointment in our collective befuddlement in the age of fake news, but we think they'd also believe in our capacity to develop solutions to what can seem like an insurmountable problem. As we explored in Chapter 4, our brains naturally seek out patterns in the world that support our own beliefs and that make us feel better about ourselves. This tendency can prove problematic to news consumers, both young and not so young, as we seek to determine what's real and what isn't in the flood of information we are all exposed to each day. The only solution is to develop some skills to help us spot suspect content—preferably *before* we've clicked on it.

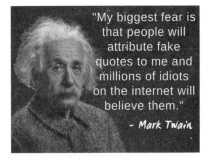

Figure 5.1 The great thing about the internet is that anyone can post just about anything, any time. The terrible thing about the internet is that anyone can post just about anything, any time—including photos of Albert Einstein next to fabricated words of wisdom, attributed to Mark Twain.

Mobile Matters

We also know that the ways in which we access news are changing. According to a Pew Research Center survey conducted in January 2018, 77% of Americans reported accessing the internet daily. Of that, 26% reported that they go online "almost constantly," up from 21% in 2015. "Younger adults are at the vanguard of the constantly connected: Roughly four-in-ten 18- to 29-year-olds (39%) now go online almost constantly and 49% go online multiple times per day." As smartphones and other mobile devices have become more widespread, roughly 83% of the time Americans spend online is accessed from their phones (Perrin & Jiang, 2018). Clearly, most of us, including our students, now use devices that fit in our pockets to both look up and discover new information. We rely on notifications to alert us to what's happening in the world. When we follow those breadcrumbs, they lead us to an ever-growing assortment of options for accessing yet more information. And this is important, because traditional methods for determining source credibility are often difficult to apply to the new ways in which we now get our news.

In the pages that follow, we're going to test your ability to sniff out fake news in the mobile environment. Whether you've spent time teaching media literacy to your students or not, some of your experience with news in other formats will no doubt serve you well here. However, we challenge you to consider how accessing information *on your phone* makes figuring out things like authority, domain, and even the date of a publication a little trickier. As adults, and particularly as educators, we have more experience than our students at determining whether or not a news story can be trusted. But is that experience keeping us from considering how tried-and-true strategies for determining a source's credibility may not apply in the same ways when we access information on a mobile device? Even if students are not allowed to use their phones when researching at school, how are we preparing them to spot suspect information when seeking out information when they're not constrained by the parameters of an assignment? More importantly, are those parameters helping them during more authentic (and potentially higher stake) information searches—or are they holding them back?

Fake News Self-Assessment

Take a look at this series of news stories as they might appear on your (or a student's) mobile device. Ultimately, we want you to label each one as being legitimate or fake, but because there's often more to the story than whether or not it's "real or fake," see what else you can answer about each potentially true piece of information. For example, pay particular attention to the app that's being used in each example and how each tool presents information differently. Additionally, if you decide that a story is fake, try to further dissect that assessment: Label the story as being a particular type of fake news, and then record some of the red flags that led you to that determination. It may not seem like it, but some of these *are* real, so take your time and examine each example carefully. You'll find an answer key later in this chapter, but in the meantime, have fun—and no cheating!

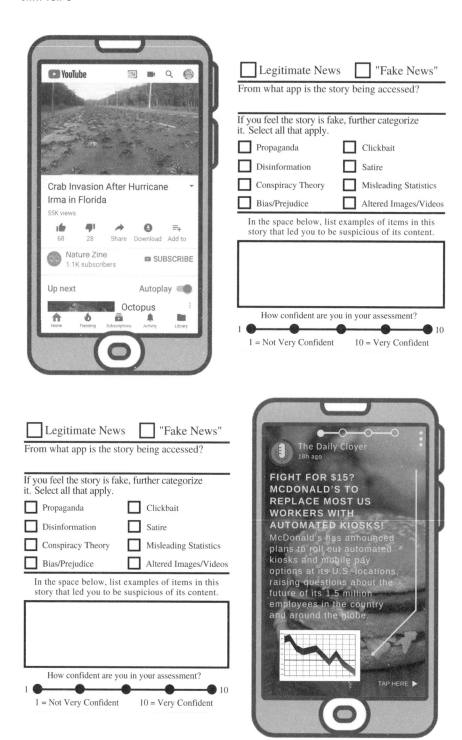

☐ Legitimate News ☐ "Fake News"

From what app is the story being accessed?

If you feel the story is fake, further categorize it. Select all that apply.

☐ Propaganda   ☐ Clickbait

☐ Disinformation   ☐ Satire

☐ Conspiracy Theory   ☐ Misleading Statistics

☐ Bias/Prejudice   ☐ Altered Images/Videos

In the space below, list examples of items in this story that led you to be suspicious of its content.

How confident are you in your assessment?

1 ●━━━●━━━●━━━●━━━● 10

1 = Not Very Confident   10 = Very Confident

☐ Legitimate News ☐ "Fake News"

From what app is the story being accessed?

If you feel the story is fake, further categorize it. Select all that apply.

☐ Propaganda   ☐ Clickbait

☐ Disinformation   ☐ Satire

☐ Conspiracy Theory   ☐ Misleading Statistics

☐ Bias/Prejudice   ☐ Altered Images/Videos

In the space below, list examples of items in this story that led you to be suspicious of its content.

How confident are you in your assessment?

1 ●━━━●━━━●━━━●━━━● 10

1 = Not Very Confident   10 = Very Confident

☐ Legitimate News   ☐ "Fake News"

From what app is the story being accessed?
_____

If you feel the story is fake, further categorize it. Select all that apply.

☐ Propaganda   ☐ Clickbait

☐ Disinformation   ☐ Satire

☐ Conspiracy Theory   ☐ Misleading Statistics

☐ Bias/Prejudice   ☐ Altered Images/Videos

In the space below, list examples of items in this story that led you to be suspicious of its content.

┌─────────────────────────────────┐
│   │
│   │
│   │
│   │
│   │
└─────────────────────────────────┘

How confident are you in your assessment?

1 ●━━━━●━━━━●━━━━●━━━━● 10

1 = Not Very Confident   10 = Very Confident

☐ Legitimate News   ☐ "Fake News"

From what app is the story being accessed?
_____

If you feel the story is fake, further categorize it. Select all that apply.

☐ Propaganda   ☐ Clickbait

☐ Disinformation   ☐ Satire

☐ Conspiracy Theory   ☐ Misleading Statistics

☐ Bias/Prejudice   ☐ Altered Images/Videos

In the space below, list examples of items in this story that led you to be suspicious of its content.

┌─────────────────────────────────┐
│   │
│   │
│   │
│   │
└─────────────────────────────────┘

How confident are you in your assessment?

1 ●━━━━●━━━━●━━━━●━━━━● 10

1 = Not Very Confident   10 = Very Confident

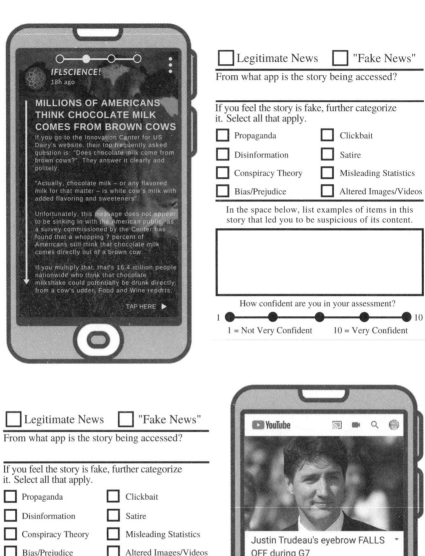

☐ Legitimate News   ☐ "Fake News"

From what app is the story being accessed?

If you feel the story is fake, further categorize it. Select all that apply.

☐ Propaganda   ☐ Clickbait

☐ Disinformation   ☐ Satire

☐ Conspiracy Theory   ☐ Misleading Statistics

☐ Bias/Prejudice   ☐ Altered Images/Videos

In the space below, list examples of items in this story that led you to be suspicious of its content.

How confident are you in your assessment?

1 ●————●————●————●————● 10
1 = Not Very Confident   10 = Very Confident

☐ Legitimate News   ☐ "Fake News"

From what app is the story being accessed?

If you feel the story is fake, further categorize it. Select all that apply.

☐ Propaganda   ☐ Clickbait

☐ Disinformation   ☐ Satire

☐ Conspiracy Theory   ☐ Misleading Statistics

☐ Bias/Prejudice   ☐ Altered Images/Videos

In the space below, list examples of items in this story that led you to be suspicious of its content.

How confident are you in your assessment?

1 ●————●————●————●————● 10
1 = Not Very Confident   10 = Very Confident

☐ Legitimate News ☐ "Fake News"

From what app is the story being accessed?

_____

If you feel the story is fake, further categorize it. Select all that apply.

☐ Propaganda   ☐ Clickbait

☐ Disinformation   ☐ Satire

☐ Conspiracy Theory   ☐ Misleading Statistics

☐ Bias/Prejudice   ☐ Altered Images/Videos

In the space below, list examples of items in this story that led you to be suspicious of its content.

How confident are you in your assessment?

1 ●━━━━●━━━━●━━━━●━━━━● 10

1 = Not Very Confident   10 = Very Confident

☐ Legitimate News ☐ "Fake News"

From what app is the story being accessed?

_____

If you feel the story is fake, further categorize it. Select all that apply.

☐ Propaganda   ☐ Clickbait

☐ Disinformation   ☐ Satire

☐ Conspiracy Theory   ☐ Misleading Statistics

☐ Bias/Prejudice   ☐ Altered Images/Videos

In the space below, list examples of items in this story that led you to be suspicious of its content.

How confident are you in your assessment?

1 ●━━━━●━━━━●━━━━● 10

1 = Not Very Confident   10 = Very Confident

Top phone (left):

67° in Springfield
Cloudy
72° / 51°
10% today

Health
Trending

Arizona woman strangles, kills rabid badger after it attacks her: "It came for my life!"

An Arizona great grandmother claims she strangled a rabid badger to death after it...

• Ferndale Flyer · 7 hr ago

Millennials

Top right form:

☐ Legitimate News ☐ "Fake News"

From what app is the story being accessed?

If you feel the story is fake, further categorize it. Select all that apply.

☐ Propaganda   ☐ Clickbait

☐ Disinformation   ☐ Satire

☐ Conspiracy Theory   ☐ Misleading Statistics

☐ Bias/Prejudice   ☐ Altered Images/Videos

In the space below, list examples of items in this story that led you to be suspicious of its content.

How confident are you in your assessment?

1 ●——●——●——● 10

1 = Not Very Confident   10 = Very Confident

Bottom left form:

☐ Legitimate News ☐ "Fake News"

From what app is the story being accessed?

If you feel the story is fake, further categorize it. Select all that apply.

☐ Propaganda   ☐ Clickbait

☐ Disinformation   ☐ Satire

☐ Conspiracy Theory   ☐ Misleading Statistics

☐ Bias/Prejudice   ☐ Altered Images/Videos

In the space below, list examples of items in this story that led you to be suspicious of its content.

How confident are you in your assessment?

1 ●——●——●——● 10

1 = Not Very Confident   10 = Very Confident

Bottom right phone:

The New Yorker
newyorker.com

THE
NEW YORKER

DEVOS SAYS TRUMP'S FORTY-PER-CENT APPROVAL RATING MEANS MORE THAN HALF OF COUNTRY SUPPORTS HIM

By Andy Borowitz February 13, 2017 12:34 PM

Fifty Historical-Dictator Puns in a Hundred and Twenty Seconds S-NAILED IT

This pun video about Donald Trump's authoritarian tendencies will really hit despot.

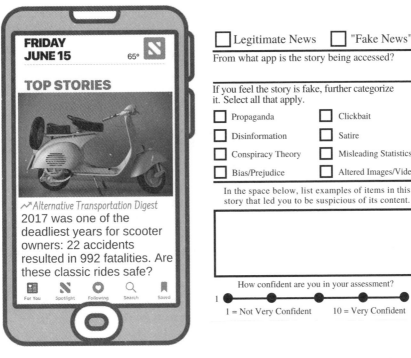

☐ Legitimate News   ☐ "Fake News"

From what app is the story being accessed?

_____

If you feel the story is fake, further categorize it. Select all that apply.

☐ Propaganda   ☐ Clickbait

☐ Disinformation   ☐ Satire

☐ Conspiracy Theory   ☐ Misleading Statistics

☐ Bias/Prejudice   ☐ Altered Images/Videos

In the space below, list examples of items in this story that led you to be suspicious of its content.

```
┌─────────────────────────────┐
│                             │
│                             │
│                             │
│                             │
└─────────────────────────────┘
```

How confident are you in your assessment?

1 ●━━●━━●━━●━━● 10

1 = Not Very Confident   10 = Very Confident

☐ Legitimate News   ☐ "Fake News"

From what app is the story being accessed?

_____

If you feel the story is fake, further categorize it. Select all that apply.

☐ Propaganda   ☐ Clickbait

☐ Disinformation   ☐ Satire

☐ Conspiracy Theory   ☐ Misleading Statistics

☐ Bias/Prejudice   ☐ Altered Images/Videos

In the space below, list examples of items in this story that led you to be suspicious of its content.

```
┌─────────────────────────────┐
│                             │
│                             │
│                             │
└─────────────────────────────┘
```

How confident are you in your assessment?

1 ●━━●━━●━━●━━● 10

1 = Not Very Confident   10 = Very Confident

Answers: Fake News Self-Assessment

Ready to check how you did? Table 5.1 lists the details on each news story.

Table 5.1 Self-Assessment Answer Key

Story	Status	App	Notes
	Fake	YouTube	This story uses a *clickbait* title and a video of another event (natural crab migration) to spread *disinformation* about a real one: Hurricane Irma. YouTube has surpassed Facebook in number of American users (Majority, 2018).
	Fake	Snapchat	This story uses a *clickbait* title and *misleading numbers* along with an unrelated graph to spread *propaganda* related to a proposed minimum wage increase. Snapchat presents news stories in ways that are often difficult to discern from advertisements.
	Fake	Twitter	This story uses a *clickbait* title to spread *propaganda* related to a real law proposing increased conservation efforts in California. Twitter is a growing news source among all age groups (Shearer and Gottfried, 2017).
	Fake	Facebook	This story uses a *clickbait* title to stoke *conspiracy theories* related to government overreach. During the last U.S. presidential election, fake news stories like this were shared more often on Facebook than legitimate news stories (Silverman, 2016).

Story	Status	App	Notes
	Real	Snapchat	This is a real story! But it still uses some *misleading statistics* to get you to click on it. Instead of saying "Only 7% of Americans believe brown cows produce chocolate milk" the authors of this story chose to lead with, "Millions of Americans" Snapchat continues to grow as a new source especially among young people (Anderson & Jiang, 2018).
	Fake	Facebook	This fake news story uses a *misleading video* to spread *disinformation* about a global leader during a highly politicized event. Although bad lighting contributed to this example, such apps as FakeApp and Lyrebird give anyone with a computer or smartphone the ability to create what are known as "*deep fakes*" or highly edited videos that make it seem as though a person has said something they really didn't (Meserole & Polyakova, 2018). YouTube has yet to come up come up with a plan for combating them (Lewis, 2018).
	Real	Instagram	This Instagram story is real. Although the numbers are incredible, they are accurate.
	Fake	YouTube	This fake story relies on a *clickbait* title and *disinformation* in the form of a *misleading image* along with reference to "hundreds of missing people" in the lead to the story in order to get people to click on it. Facebook has recently implemented an "about this article" feature that allows users to learn more about the sources of information before clicking (Lewsing, 2018).

Story	Status	App	Notes
	Fake	Google (News Alerts)	This fake story uses a *clickbait* title and a *manipulated image* (to depict a rabid badger) in order to spread *disinformation*. Google and similar apps allow users to create news notifications that are tailored to them based on their browsing habits along with user selections. The result is the mobile version of a filter bubble.
	Fake	Browser (such as Safari)	This fake news story is an example of *satire*, or actual fake news. Although satirical news sites identify themselves as such, they are often shared like legitimate news stories, particularly when the fake headlines parallel existing *conspiracy theories* (Woolf, 2016).
	Fake	Apple News Alerts	This fake news story uses *disinformation* in the form of *misleading statistics* to make readers think scooters are unsafe. Even if the numbers in the story are true, they are presented outside of the context of other years or even the total number of scooter owners. Apple News and similar apps allow users to create news notifications that are tailored to them based on their browsing habits along with user selections.
	Real	Instagram	This story is real. Brrrr!

So ... How Did You Do?

Our goal in creating this resource was not to trick anyone but to illustrate some fundamental truths about how the way we access news should change the way we talk to students about evaluating it. Here are some things that struck us as we've been researching this topic and working with educators:

- Content looks different on our phones than it does on a more traditional device.

- Even something as simple as figuring out the URL/domain of web-based content can require a couple of extra steps on a phone compared to looking at the same piece of information on a computer.

- From a mobile device, the ads in apps look much more like actual content, and it can be trickier to make them go away without clicking on them.

- Unlike for computer-based browsers, ad blockers for mobile devices basically do not exist yet (Claburn 2017).

- Research shows that students don't seek news as much as news comes to them through self-created notification algorithms. Our media literacy programs should be addressing skills for developing reliable news feeds.

- The vast majority of educators did not learn to research using mobile devices and will likely need support in shifting traditional media literacy lessons to include how today's learners get their news outside of school.

Table 5.2 lists a few other online fake news self-assessments that we like and thought might be useful for you and your students. We've also included a digital version of our assessment, which you are welcome to share with your students and staff. (Remember, URLs that are truncated using Bitly are case sensitive!)

Table 5.2 Other Online Fake News Self-Assessments

Resource	Source	Description	Access
Factitious	JoLT: A collaboration between American University's GameLab and School of Communication	You can view stories with or without their sources or source before choosing fake or real.	bit.ly/2JKUbFN
Can You Spot the Fake News Story?	Houghton Mifflin Harcourt's Channel One News: An award-winning daily news program that encourages young people to become informed, global citizens	This quick quiz tests your ability to pick a fake news story from a real one. Be sure to scroll down for access to several lesson plans related to fake news.	bit.ly/2JKUTCX
Can You Spot Fake News?	Penguin Books: Publisher of trade books in the United States	Inspired by the book *A Field Guide to Lies and Statistics* by Daniel Levitin, this quiz focuses on the ways statistics and "dodgy science" are used to mislead.	bit.ly/2JTwlra
Can You Spot the Fake News Stories	BBC News Service, British Broadcasting Corporation: the world's largest public broadcasting service	This is an interesting take on how fake news in the U.S. is viewed in Great Britain.	bbc.in/2JUDSX2

Resource	Source	Description	Access
Real or Fake?	PundiFact: A fact-checking website that rates the accuracy of claims by elected officials and others who speak up in American politics	Rather than present example news stories for you to evaluate, this quiz asks about the attributes of a story you've found elsewhere, and then warns of potential warning signs.	bit.ly/2JUDYOo
Our Fake News Self-Assessment		Google Forms version of our Fake News Self-Assessment.	bit.ly/FvsFSelf_ AssessmentCOPY

In the next chapter, we'll be exploring tools and resources that we think offer excellent starting points for helping educators tackle the topic of fake news and media literacy in their classrooms, libraries, and computer labs. Many of the resources you'll find there were recommended by educators. That said, most are grounded in traditional research approaches using desktops, laptops, or Chromebooks, which are still important and useful tools for both teachers and students. As you explore them, however, we hope you'll consider how some might be adapted to include a mobile device component.

1. How did you do on the Fake News Self-Assessment? What surprised you most about your results? What next steps will you take to continue your own learning in this area?

2. Rate your current media literacy program in terms of how you feel it prepares today's learners to access and evaluate information *their* way?

One Bar:
Weak Signal

Three Bars:
Getting There

Five Bars:
Signal Is Strong

3. Tweet us! We want to know how your students or colleagues did on the Fake News Self-Assessment! What kinds of conversations arose from using this tool with other learners or educators?

CHAPTER 6

All Is Not Lost! Resources for Combatting Fake News

Our "digital natives" may be able to flit between Facebook and Twitter while simultaneously uploading a selfie to Instagram and texting a friend. But when it comes to evaluating information that flows through social media channels, they are easily duped.

—The Stanford History Education Group, "Evaluating Information:
The Cornerstone of Civic Online Reasoning"

B etween January 2015 and June 2016, researchers at Stanford University's Stanford History Education Group (SHEG) undertook the task of evaluating how well students across the country could evaluate online sources of information. To do this, they administered 56 tasks to middle and high school students across 12 states, collecting responses from more than 7,800 students.

The results were both shocking and disappointing. Over and over again, students failed to effectively evaluate the credibility of information from a variety of sources and in a variety of formats. According to the researchers, students who participated displayed "stunning and dismaying consistency" in their responses, failing to demonstrate even basic-level fact-checking abilities. In addition to not being able to pick out advertisements from actual content, students from all age groups trusted manipulated images, failed to see bias within content, and trusted fake accounts over real ones (SHEG, 2016).

The Stanford researchers also shared what they'd gleaned about the factors present in many schools that made the results of their study possible:

> None of this is rocket science. But it's often not taught in school. In fact, some schools have special filters that direct students to already vetted sites, effectively creating a generation of bubble children who never develop the immunities needed to ward off the toxins that float across their Facebook feeds, where students most often get their news. This approach protects young people from the real world rather than preparing them to deal with it. (Wineburg, 2016)

Ultimately, we think there are many lessons to be gleaned from the Stanford study. In addition to publishing their methods and findings, Stanford researchers also shared many of the sample tasks given to students. These resources can be used to help educators establish a baseline of student understanding, which in turn, can help them develop an action plan for moving forward. As the Stanford researchers rightly pointed out, the ball is in our court:

> Never have we had so much information at our fingertips. Whether this bounty will make us smarter and better informed or more ignorant and narrow-minded will depend on our awareness of this problem and our educational response to it. (SHEG, 2016)

It's Complicated, but Not Impossible.

Perhaps one of Facebook's numerous status options best sums up our relationship with news and our ability to discern what's real and what isn't: It's complicated. No longer do we have to go out and look for news. Increasingly, the news comes to us on our mobile devices 24/7 through a series of personalized notifications that we either very intentionally set up ourselves or that are created for us based on our browsing histories and online behavior. Our efforts to determine credibility are further confounded by the reality that these feeds consist of content created by a complex mix of professional and citizen journalists, satirists, conspiracy theorists, online trolls, and people who make their living by writing intentionally fake and often deeply biased news stories that exist solely to fool us. New apps that allow "deep fake" alterations to existing images or videos enable everyday users to further blur the lines between what's real and what isn't. One thing that *is* clear, however, is that as long as content creators continue to experience big paydays from the pay-per-click advertising by which search engines and social media create revenue, the chase for viral content—real or fake—will go on.

We're not convinced that a foolproof system of determining source credibility ever existed. Because news stories have never been simply real or fake, no mnemonic device or clever four-step solution for spotting fake news will ever prove infallible against the plethora of ways information can be manipulated to further an agenda or simply perpetrate a hoax. Today more than ever, decisions about what we can believe and what we should be suspicious of are increasingly complex—kind of ironic, considering the current narrative, which reduces an incredibly nuanced and complicated problem to a single, easy-to-apply label of *fake news*, suggesting that credibility should be a snap to determine. And, of course, this is part of the problem. The more advanced and subtle information manipulation becomes, the more in-depth and multifaceted our strategies for foiling it must be. We can no longer point to any source and guarantee that its information is 100% accurate and without bias. We must teach our students to deconstruct media, in all its forms, and to uncover any underlying messaging. As Joyce Valenza wrote in 2016, we must teach students to

> interrogate their sources. [We] must update our own skill sets and toolkits to guide students in navigating a growingly nuanced universe of news. We must also examine and recognize our own biases so that we are open to contrary and conflicting ideas. This is our banner to wave, our curriculum to co-teach.

In short, this problem is multifaceted. So too must be the solution.

Although we're not claiming to have all the answers, "we do know some people," as the saying goes. One of the benefits of living during a time of extreme connectedness is the ability to use the same tools by which we access other information to create personal learning networks (PLNs). These networks help us learn about emerging practices and share our own experiences. When faced with a problem as intricate as media literacy, it helps to have a tribe on your side. We truly cannot do this work alone. Luckily, we do not have to. Over the years, and with the help of our own PLNs, we've curated lists of resources to use and share with the educators we work with. We've sorted these resources into several categories and share them now with you as a collection of tools to add to your toolkit.

Frameworks and Tips for Determining Credibility

The resources listed in Table 6.1 are examples of protocols or tips to help students evaluate information. They are designed to capture the attention of our learners while also being easy to remember. Whether you use one of these or create your own, a framework like those included in Table 6.1 can help students develop evaluation strategies that can be applied across media.

Table 6.1 Tools for Evaluating Credibility

Resource	Grade Levels	Description	Access
Library Girl's Tips for Spotting Fake News *(Source: Jennifer LaGarde)*	ES +	Infographic to help students evaluate a news story.	bit.ly/tips4spotting fakenews
How to Spot Fake News *(Source: IFLA)*	ES +	Infographic to help students evaluate a news story.	bit.ly/2JZsCIX

Resource	Grade Levels	Description	Access
5 Ways to Spot Fake News *(Source: Common Sense Media)*	ES+	Video outlining five tips to help students evaluate news sources.	bit.ly/2KadSGW
CARS Checklist for Evaluating Internet Sources *(Source: Andy Spinks)*	ES +	List of questions to help students evaluate information.	bit.ly/CARSchecklist
Is This Story Share-Worthy? Flowchart *(Source: NewseumED)*	ES +	Infographic to help students evaluate information by deciding if it is something they would endorse by sharing with others.	bit.ly/2I2CUD5
Five Ws of Website Evaluation *(Source: Cathy Schrock)*	Upper ES +	List of questions to help students evaluate information. Questions are modeled after the "five Ws" often used by journalists.	bit.ly/2K1tjBw

Resource	Grade Levels	Description	Access
How to Fact Check with Google Using Reverse Image Search (Source: Common Sense Education)	Upper ES +	Video with tips for using Google's reverse image search to help students evaluate information.	http://bit.ly/2LCMwpy
Web Evaluation: Does This Website Smell Funny to You? (Source: AASL)	Upper ES +	List of questions, called the FART Test, to help students evaluate a website. Created to compliment the CRAAP Test protocol.	bit.ly/2K2KHWo
The CRAAP Test (Source: Meriam Library, California State University, Chico)	MS	List of questions to help students evaluate information.	bit.ly/2K2K1jO
Here's How to Outsmart Fake News in Your Facebook Feed (Source: CNN)	MS +	Series of recommendations from journalists to help students recognize suspect news stories.	cnn.it/2I2A7K7

Resource	Grade Levels	Description	Access
10 Ways to Spot a Fake News Article *(Source: EasyBib)*	MS +	List of questions to help students evaluate information.	bit.ly/2K6PJkw
Evaluating a News Article *(Source: EasyBib)*	MS +	Infographic to help students evaluate a news story.	bit.ly/2K7en4C
Fact Check Like a Pro *(Source: Indiana University East)*	MS +	Infographic to help students evaluate a news story.	bit.ly/2K7eDkf
The Problem with Fake News and How Our Students Can Solve It *(Source: John Spencer)*	MS +	Video with tips, called the Five Cs of Critical Consuming, for helping students evaluate a new story.	bit.ly/2K5014H

Resource	Grade Levels	Description	Access
How to Spot Fake News *(Source: FactCheck.org)*	MS +	Video with tips for helping students evaluate a new story.	bit.ly/2JZynGz
Introducing IMVAIN *(Source: Center for News Literacy)*	MS +	Set of tips with an acronym mnemonic to help students evaluate a news story.	bit.ly/2K17HoG
Evaluating Sources: Using the RADAR Framework *(Source: William H. Hannon Library, Loyola Marymount University)*	HS	List of questions, targeting older students, to help them evaluate information.	bit.ly/2K2tE6M
Top Six Red Flags that Identify a Conspiracy Theory Article *(Source: Vanessa Otero)*	HS	Series of tips to help older students identify a conspiracy theory within a news story or article.	bit.ly/2I1fUnT

Resource	Grade Levels	Description	Access
The Future of Fake News *Source: Edutopia*	HS	List of five essential questions to help students identify bias in a news story.	https://edut.to/2wui1Nl

Sample Lesson Plans

The resources in Table 6.2 are examples of lessons created by educators from around the world who have found success in helping students discern fact from fiction in the news they consume. Rich with supplemental materials, many of these lesson plans could be adapted to meet the needs of a wide variety of learners.

Table 6.2 Sample Lesson Plans

Resource	Grade Levels	Description	Access
I Taught My 5th Graders How to Spot Fake News. Now They Won't Stop Fact Checking Me. *(Source: Vox)*	Upper ES +	Article by Scott Bedley that contains a lesson used with fifth-grade students.	bit.ly/2K6HUva

Resource	Grade Levels	Description	Access
Supermoons Cause Tidal Waves—True or False? *(Source: School Library Journal)*	Upper ES	News literacy program for fourth graders.	bit.ly/2I3kdz4
Educator Toolkit: News & Media Literacy *(Source: Common Sense Media)*	ES +	Curricula including lesson plans for all grade levels.	bit.ly/2K3uQa6
Facts vs. Opinions vs. Informed Opinions and Their Role in Journalism *(Source: Common Sense Education)*	ES+	Activities for determining the difference between the opinions and facts, as well as encourage critical thinking.	bit.ly/2wwNmit
How to Choose Your News *(Source: TED-Ed)*	MG +	Customizable lesson and accompanying video on how news is reported and how to evaluate it for accuracy and bias.	bit.ly/2K0qsbU

Resource	Grade Levels	Description	Access
Evaluating Sources in a "Post-Truth" World: Ideas for Teaching and Learning About Fake News *(Source: The New York Times)*	MG +	Multipart lesson with ideas, questions, and resources for teaching about fake news; linked version for ELL students.	nyti.ms/2K1j00i
Curriculum and Lessons *(Source: University of Missouri School of Journalism)*	MG +	Hundreds of lesson plans and resources related to journalism, news literacy, and civic education; for students and teachers.	bit.ly/2K2rYdn
Lesson Plan: How to Teach Your Students About Fake News *(Source: PBS)*	MS +	Warm-up, main, and extension activities aimed to help students to navigate the media and evaluate news.	to.pbs.org/2K1XS6T
Fact or Fiction? 8 TED-Ed Videos and a TED Talk to Show to Your Students *(Source: TED-Ed)*	MS +	Lessons for helping you teach students about about fake news.	bit.ly/8TEDed_fake newsvids

Resource	Grade Levels	Description	Access
Media Literacy & Fake News—A Lesson Plan *(Source: C-Span)*	MS +	Five videos, including one from the satirical site, *The Onion*, as well as questions that challenge learners to consider the reasons why someone might want to create a fake news story.	bit.ly/2K51W9p
Critical Evaluation of a Web Page *(Source: Kathy Schrock)*	MS +	Materials, including an intentionally bogus website, that encourage students to use brainstorming to create their own protocol for spotting suspicious information online.	bit.ly/2K2URmJ
3 Fast Free Lesson Plans for Fighting Fake News *(Source: Vicki Davis)*	MS +	Three quick "bell ringer" activities to help students consider ways to identify suspicious content online.	bit.ly/2I5slPw
Lesson Plan: Fighting Fake News *(Source: KQED)*	HS	Resources, prompts, and activities to help students to determine the consequences of fake news becoming widespread and to evaluate news stories.	bit.ly/2K768po

Resource	Grade Levels	Description	Access
Hoax or No Hoax? Strategies for Online Comprehension and Evaluation *(Source: Read Write Think)*	HS	A multisession unit designed to help students develop strategies for identifying hoax news stories from real ones.	bit.ly/2K45UPU
Fake News *(Source: Nearpod)*	HS	Activities and resources to help students consider the effect of fake news on society and develop strategies for identifying suspicious news stories; includes both a pre- and post-lesson assessment.	bit.ly/2JZR3CA

Fact-Checking Tools and Other Useful Resources

The resources in Table 6.3 are examples of tools that can be used to determine if a news story or website has already been debunked or otherwise identified as containing suspect information. We recommend using these resources with students who are in middle school or older. Meanwhile, Table 6.4 includes some additional resources to help students from elementary to high school become skilled soldiers in the fight against fake news!

Table 6.3 Tools for Fact Checking Content

Resource	Description	Access
FactCheck.Org	FactCheck.org is a project of the Annenberg Public Policy Center of the University of Pennsylvania.	www.factcheck.org
Snopes.com	Debunking for more than twenty years, Snopes.com has come to be regarded as an online touchstone for research on rumors and misinformation. (See the sidebar, "A Word About Snopes.com.")	bit.ly/2K66e0A
Whois Lookup	DomainTools offers this search site as a way to learn more about a website based on its domain or IP address.	whois.domaintools.com
Hoax-Slayer	Besides debunking and publishing educational articles on hoaxes and scams, this site provides a resource where you can search to check the veracity of email and social media messages.	bit.ly/2K7vvHo

Resource	Description	Access
Fact Checker	This online column from *The Washington Post* newspaper provides "the truth behind the rhetoric."	wapo.st/2K2I3jq
FotoForensics	This site enables you to submit an image to determine if it has been manipulated.	www.fotoforensics.com

Table 6.4 Potpourri: Other Useful Resources for Combatting Fake News

Resource	Grade Levels	Description	Access
Checkology *(Source: The News Literacy Project)*	ES +	Online learning management system designed to equip students with the tools to evaluate and interpret the news.	checkology.org

Resource	Grade Levels	Description	Access
NewseumED *(Source: Newseum)*	ES +	Collection of learning tools on media literacy and the First Amendment.	newseumed.org
Linkbait Title Generator *(Source: Content Row)*	ES +	Tool that gives students the chance to practice generating their own clickbait headlines.	bit.ly/clickbaitgenerator
How Savvy Are Your Students? 7 Fake Websites to Really Test Their Evaluation Skills *(Source: EasyBib)*	ES +	Collection of hoax websites to use with students.	bit.ly/2K96ADG
Tackling Fake News: Strategies for Teaching Media Literacy *(Source: Scholastic)*	ES +	Collection of resources and lessons for helping students sharpen their media literacy skills.	bit.ly/2K4Qfje

Resource	Grade Levels	Description	Access
Break Your Own News *(Source: Jonathan Cresswell)*	MS +	Site that allows students to create their own "breaking news" story featuring tactics frequently used by creators of fake news.	bit.ly/2K0XhlQ
Bad News *(Source: Cambridge University)*	MS +	Online game that allows students to make decisions about contributing to the spread of fake news.	bit.ly/2I5KNaJ
Quiz: How Well Can You Tell Factual from Opinion Statements? *(Source: Pew Research Center)*	MS +	Quiz that allows students and educators to see how their own biases affect their ability to discern fact from opinion in the news.	pewrsr.ch/2K2Y59P
Center for News Literacy *(Source: Stony Brook University)*	MS +	Collection of resources designed to help teach students how to use critical thinking skills to judge the reliability and credibility of news reports and news sources.	bit.ly/2JYpKMe

Resource	Grade Levels	Description	Access
List of Satirical News Websites *(Source: Wikipedia)*	MS +	Crowdsourced list of hoax websites.	bit.ly/2K48jdf
Fake News. It's Complicated *(Source: Harvard University's John F. Kennedy School of Government)*	MS +	Collection of resources to help students identify the different types of false information they may encounter.	bit.ly/2K1XchR
Media Bias Chart *(Source: Vanessa Ortero)*	HS +	Resource for helping students and educators identify bias within widely used news sources. *(Note: This chart is updated frequently, so a search for the latest version may be necessary.)*	bit.ly/2LCznNm
False, Misleading, Clickbait-y, and/ or Satirical "News" Sources *(Source: Melissa Zimdars, Merrimack College)*	HS +	List of strategies, definitions, and news sources that have been identified as false or misleading.	bit.ly/fakenews_doc

Resource	Grade Levels	Description	Access
Reverse Image Search (Source: TinEye)	HS +	Resource that helps students track an image online.	www.tineye.com
Hoaxy: Visualize Spread of Claims and Fact Checking (Source: Indiana University)	HS +	Tool to help students visualize how a false news story spreads across platforms.	bit.ly/2Kad6K2
The News Literacy Project (Source: News Literacy Project)	Educators	Collection of resources for educators who are dedicated to helping students strengthen their media literacy skills.	newslit.org/about
Media Education Lab (Source: University of Rhode Island)	Educators	Collection of resources for educators designed to improve media literacy education.	bit.ly/2K4qAaq

Resource	Grade Levels	Description	Access
Mind Over Media: Analyzing Contemporary Propaganda *(Source: Renee Hobbs and the United States Holocaust Memorial Museum)*	Educators	Collection of resources for educators designed to help students recognize propaganda.	bit.ly/2K0M9sm
13 Tips for Teaching News and Information Literacy *(Source: School Library Journal)*	Educators	Article and tips for educators to help them equip their students with media literacy skills.	bit.ly/2K1lD27
The Sift: An Educator's Guide to the Week in News Literacy *(Source: The News Literacy Project)*	Educators	Online newsletter for educators to help them identify opportunities for media literacy instruction within that week's news headlines.	bit.ly/2K3TXtw
Do You Know All You Should About "News" Feeds, Click Bait, and Credible Sources?" *(Source: Young Adult Library Services Association; YALSA)*	Educators	Article for educators that challenges them (with tips) to sharpen their own skills at identifying suspect content online.	bit.ly/2K45QzC

A Word About Snopes.com

We are aware that there has been controversy surrounding Snopes.com and its political neutrality or perceived lack thereof. That said, researchers and trained journalists continue to use Snopes, because as an article published in 2017 by the American Press Institute described, Snopes' fact checking continues to revolve around several critical features:

Sources: The sites and statistics used to investigate the statement or rumor.

Authors: Who wrote the article?

Dates: When the investigation was published and when it was updated.

Original claim: Precisely when, where, and what was said, with plenty of context.

Clear verdict: You won't leave without knowing whether the claim was true, false, or just not provable.

Brevity: You don't need to wade through a 1,000-word treatise to find out how that verdict was reached.

Reader involvement: Snopes actively asks for reader tips and offers a newsletter. (Elizabeth, 2017)

This is not to say that Snopes, or any other fact-checking site, is above scrutiny. As long as its practices continue to adhere to standards reflected in the industry, however, we continue to see it as a credibility resource. Remember, too, there are lots of other options (listed in this chapter's tables), and it never hurts to check more than one fact checker when determining credibility and forming an opinion.

The Notification Generation

We've personally vetted all of the resources in this chapter, or they have been highly recommended to us by other educators, who have used them with their students. That said, one of the things you may have noticed about them is that none specifically address how applying these strategies may be different when students access news on their phones or tablets. Let's be clear: The basics of fact checking don't change, regardless of what device you're using. No matter how the information is being accessed, it's obvious that consuming news can no longer be a passive activity. Over time, for better or worse, the job of journalists and content creators has changed. No longer is their role to simply research a story and then present it to the public in the clearest, most thorough and neutral way possible. In the 24-hour news cycle, in which legitimate journalists compete with anyone with a phone, their job descriptions now also include the critical functions of getting the story first *and* getting more people to click on their version of it than on competing versions. Which means that our jobs as news consumers must change too. No longer can we just take what is presented to us at face value.

A News Consumer's Skill Set

Spend any time at all immersed in the resources shared in this chapter and some themes emerge. As news consumers in a world where platforms change constantly, and where virality is too often valued as much as accuracy, our skill set must include the ability to recognize:

- **Our own biases.** We must be aware of the personal and implicit bias that we all bring to any piece of information. Further, we must recognize how that baggage leads us to more easily accept stories that confirm what we already agree with or think to be true.

- **Clickbait.** Although these tactics evolve, we need to hone our nonsense detectors such that we become naturally suspicious whenever we see:

  > Sensationalist headlines
  > Vague or incomplete statistics
  > Reporting that seeks to stoke emotion
  > Images that appear gratuitous or that don't make sense in context

- **Authority in authorship.** Because so much of what we consume as news comes to us from social media, it's tempting to trust that because our Uncle Frank or our best friend posted something, it must be true. We'll touch more on this later, but we have to help our students recognize that authority must be found in the originator of the content, not the individual who shared it.

֍ **The necessity of triangulation.** The very best way to know if a story is true is to determine where it came from, and then to look for other credible resources that back it up. Although this extra step can seem like a bridge too far in a world where we now can just shout at devices in our home that will then turn on the lights, adjust the room temperature, or order something online, it really isn't optional. If we care about whether information is accurate, we're going to have to put in a little work.

As important as it is to be vigilant when evaluating news from any source, we must also keep in mind that news looks different when it's accessed on our phones. Considering the use of mobile devices for news access is on the rise (Pew, 2017), we feel it's critical that media literacy efforts begin to include additional support for helping students (and teachers) leverage these tools and their features in the most effective way possible.

To do this, we must first allow students to use these devices as research tools in school. Our kids research information all the time—from the latest video game cheats to what people are saying about their favorite musician or YouTube star. And speaking of YouTube, the kids we teach now are far more influenced by content creators on YouTube than by more traditional celebrities. They also see being a YouTuber as a potential career option (Ault, 2015). Although the vast majority of YouTubers struggle to make a living from their videos, the lavish lifestyles of those who have hit it big continue to inspire kids to follow in their digital footprints (Bloomberg, 2018). And this matters.

As our students continue to use their phones to gather information outside of school, and as they continue to be greatly influenced by the content creators in those spaces, a disconnect between the skills we know are necessary to help them think critically about information only grows wider when the opportunities we provide them to practice those skills don't look or feel authentic. To whatever degree possible, we have to give our students the chance to evaluate news and information at school in the same ways they do it in every other location.

What's more, we need to allow, or even encourage, learners to use the apps and information sources they employ outside of school as potentially cited resources in school. What's the danger in letting students cite a Snap, Tweet, or Instagram post if we've emphasized fact checking as part of the research process? If we really want our students to apply a healthy level of skepticism to all information both in and out of school, we need to remove any barrier that prevents them from seeing how the skills we require they demonstrate during instruction apply even when their teachers are not around.

Notification Curators

As part of those instructional efforts, we must also add the goal of teaching learners to be notification curators to our existing media literacy objectives. When the Knight Foundation interviewed young people about their news consumption habits, researchers found that instead of actively seeking new information, for many, news was delivered to them through notifications. "The first thing I do when I wake up is check my phone. Like I wake up, turn my alarm off, check my phone [And] I'll have notifications . . ." reported one participant in the study. (We can relate to this daily habit and we're betting many of you can, too.) Others in the study said they found the barrage of notifications stressful (Knight, 2016). As educators, we have to ask ourselves how our current media literacy programs support the needs of the "notification generation." And if the answer to that question falls short, we need to be willing to rethink our strategy.

Here are a few ways that we can guide our students in becoming more effective users of their phones and tablets as devices for accessing information, including some tips for helping them become better managers of their notifications:

> ♀ **Help kids become experts at curating their notifications.**
> Teach them the steps for identifying which apps have permission
> to send them notifications. Once they know what's on that list,

teach them to scrutinize the apps they allow to push information towards them in the same vigorous way they would resources for an assignment. Vanessa Ortero's "Media Bias Chart" (see Table 6.4) and similar tools can be valuable in helping kids and adults alike make sure their notifications are filled with both accurate and balanced information. Although managing notifications can be helpful in reducing frequent interruptions of their arrival, *curating* notifications is a different skill. It's important that our students understand that they have a great deal of control over *which* information is pushed towards them through notifications. We must arm them with the skills to curate notifications that are populated by the most credible sources available and that expose our learners to a variety of viewpoints.

- **Provide kids with some strategies for cutting through the noise when accessing information on their phones.** Although mobile ad blockers are not widely available, some browser apps (Safari for iOS and Firefox or Edge for Android) offer Reader View, which allow users to peruse content without distractions from ads, videos, sponsored content links, and so on. Note how

Figure 6.1 Compare reading a news story on a phone in Reader View (left) versus in the ad-filled default view.

in Figure 6.1 the same story below looks different when viewed on reader view versus the default view. This is an effective way for kids to focus on the information first and to apply content related fact-checking strategies without being distracted by all the other junk.

⚲ **Teach kids how to delete their app browsing history.** One way to interrupt the filter bubble effect (the ways the internet tailors our experiences based on our browsing history) is to delete that history from time to time. Even if we are keenly aware of the biases we bring to the table when assessing information sources, internet algorithms can prove a barrier between our good intentions and access to a broad array of viewpoints. Tidying up your browsing history from time to time may mean that you occasionally have to re-enter a password, but the benefits outweigh any inconvenience.

⚲ **Teach kids to care more about who authored the information than about who shared it.** In a news landscape driven by social media, authority has become a layered and complex thing. Although we may recognize that the person in our network sharing a news story is not the original source of the information, their endorsement of it matters—even though it really shouldn't. What's more, the sharer's identity gives many people (young and not-so-young) unjustified confidence in the information's credibility (Anderson & Rainie, 2017). It is true that social media networks, including Facebook and Twitter, have announced plans to combat fake news on their sites; however, the onus ultimately lies with us to make sure we don't further spread misleading or biased information by sharing the stuff our friends post without additionally vetting it. We have to help our students recognize that the only authority that matters is that of the original source. Our friends or relatives may be endorsing a news source by reposting it, but that endorsement is not enough.

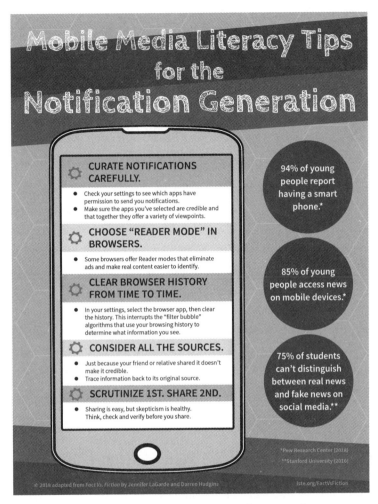

Figure 6.2 Today's teacher-librarians are ready! Are you?

⚲ **Encourage our students to scrutinize first and share second (if at all).** One of the things that may make accessing information on our phones preferable to other methods is the ease by which we can share it, almost effortlessly, with other people and across multiple platforms. But as Uncle Ben told Peter Parker in the movie *Spider-Man* (2002), "With great power comes great responsibility." Put another way, just because we *can* share something, doesn't mean we *should*. Our students, like all students before them, are social creatures. Convincing them to not share everything they create or come in contact with may feel like an uphill battle, but it's one worth fighting, especially when in the context of mobile media literacy. NewseumED's "Is This Story Shareworthy?" infographic and accompanying lessons (see Tables 6.1 and 6.2) and similar tools are great resources for helping kids learn to apply this filter to the way they choose to endorse information by sharing it (NewseumED, 2017).

There's an old saying that goes, "What gets observed, gets done." Although it refers to the belief that people are most productive when they think someone is watching or evaluating them, it also speaks to the idea that visual reminders can be helpful tools for achieving goals. After all, as another old saying goes, "Out of sight, out of mind." To provide a visual reminder of strategies to help students use their mobile devices more effectively as news consumers, we created the infographic shown in Figure 6.2. You can download and print your own color version by going to the book's product page at iste.org/FactVsFiction. Post it in your classroom or library to provide a visual cue to anyone who walks through the door that this is an issue you care about and are working on with students. We hope you find it helpful.

It's a Bird! It's a Plane! It's Your Teacher-Librarian!

In 2011, Jennifer created the flyer shown in Figure 6.3 to illustrate the changing role of the teacher-librarian. Growing concern over the perceived irrelevance of librarians, coupled with the elimination of these positions in school districts across the country, proved a powerful source of inspiration for trying to spread the word about how this role had evolved over the years. Now, seven years later, stereotypes about teacher-librarians and their value to teachers and students still exist, but the need for these professionals in schools and in the lives of young people is greater than ever. In addition to their function as reading role models and cultivators of dynamic and diverse library collections, teacher-librarians are the original information specialists.

Figure 6.3 Wonder Twin powers—activate! Today's school librarians are ready to help you tackle media literacy for the digital age with students.

Degreed teacher-librarians are highly trained information conduits that connect students and teachers to the best sources of information, helping both become independent researchers and evaluators of that information. At the same time, teacher-librarians support students and teachers as they grow as creators of credible information sources themselves. Plus, teacher-librarians work with all of the students in the building and possess an understanding of curricula that transcends content areas.

All of this to say that classroom teachers and teacher-librarians are an unbeatable team in the fight against fake news. Although it is true that teacher-librarians can (and do) teach this content during fixed library lessons or times when teachers sign up to bring their classes to the library, the real potential for instructional magic lies in collaboration. Here are just a few things teacher-librarians can do as a partner in teaching media literacy:

- Identify potential **opportunities within content standards** to integrate media literacy in authentic ways.

- Identify **digital and print resources** that support both content and media literacy learning.

- **Co-teach alongside classroom teachers** to provide students with two adult resources as they explore, experiment, and tackle new challenges.

- **Help manage** the use of **technology as a learning tool.**

- **Make connections** between the lesson being taught and what students are learning in other classes.

- Help connect students and teachers to other learners and experts to **extend the learning beyond the four walls** of the classroom.

- Assist in **evaluating student products** and **coach students** towards improvement.

- Help teachers **reflect on and evaluate the effectiveness of the media literacy** lesson after the fact, so that next time it can be even better.

Although teaching media literacy is not solely the teacher-librarian's job, it is in their core skills. Given the challenges teachers sometimes cite as preventing them from tackling media literacy as part of their instruction, why wouldn't you want to join forces with someone who was specifically trained to meet these challenges head on? Yes, school librarians certainly do check out books and help transform your students into adults whose lives are empowered and informed by story, but they are also ready and willing to be your partner in preparing these same young learners to navigate a world that constantly bombards them with information.

As we end this chapter, we hope the big takeaway is that the greatest resource we have in tackling this work is each other. In the next chapter you'll see how other educators have harnessed the power of some of the resources listed here, along with the support of colleagues (both in an out of their buildings), to create meaningful learning experiences for students. Fake news doesn't stand a chance against the awesome power of teachers and librarians whose students are armed with the skills necessary to defeat it.

Chapter 6 _____

1. Which of the resources from this chapter do you plan to share with other educators? In what way can one (or more) of the resources you learned about in this chapter be used with the learners you work with?

2. What are some ways that you can evolve your media literacy program to include skills that are appropriate for the "notification generation?"

3. Tweet us! In what ways are classroom teachers and teacher-librarians in your school or district working together to tackle the issue of fake news with students and staff? Share your success stories along with areas of growth!

Voices from the Field

I t's very difficult to quantify the number of fake news sites that exist, because of the many categories that fake news falls under and the organic nature of fake news itself. As we've discussed in previous chapters, unless you're talking about pure satire, like in *The Onion* or *The Oatmeal*, very few sites or articles are 100% fake. This is because purveyors of false information know that sprinkling in at least a few facts, among other misleading or fabricated material, accomplishes two things: It makes readers more likely to deem the entire work credible and makes the job more difficult for fact-checking websites to label the entire story or site as fake. What we do know, however, is that as long as creators of fake news continue to earn revenue from creating false content, the problem will only continue to grow at immeasurable rates.

The Answer Is in the Lily Pads

Naturally, this begs the question: how can a finite number of educators tackle a problem of seemingly infinite proportions? One way to look at it is through the lens of the lily pad riddle, which goes something like this: Imagine a pond with one lily pad in it. Every day the number of lily pads in the pond doubles—2, 4, 8, 16, 32, and so on. If on day 30 the pond is completely full, on which day was it half full?

As Brent Esplin wrote on his blog, the most common answer is day fifteen. "Our mind automatically goes to this answer because we are comfortable with linear thinking. If the lily pad covers the entire pond in 30 days, it must cover half the pond in 15 days" (2016).

But, of course, that's not the answer. If the number of lily pads doubles each day, and it is completely full on day 30, then it would be half full on day 29. Esplin goes on to challenge his readers to estimate how much of the pond would actually be covered on day 15. As he explained, "The correct answer is that the lily pad will only have covered .0031% (3 thousandths of one percent) of the pond on day 15. In fact, the lily pad will only cover more than one percent of the pond on day 24" (2016).

We struggle with this riddle because it requires us to think exponentially instead of linearly. And that's part of what makes the task of preparing kids for the media literacy challenges of today so difficult. Fake news grows at an exponential rate, not a linear one, which can make it tough for us to wrap our brains around it.

But what the lily pad riddle doesn't account for is how growth is affected by environment. Surely, drought, pollutants, or a loss of food source would affect the growth of lily pads. And this is where we come in. Although the motivations of individual fake news creators varies, it can be said that financial gain is at the heart of what keeps many toiling at their keyboards. Because we know that more clicks, Likes, and shares equate to more revenue, our power lies in cultivating thinking that keeps people from providing those clicks. In other words, we may not be able to control the number of people who choose to create fake news, but we *can* work to affect their food source. Many educators are already doing just that.

When we decided to tackle a book on the topic of fake news and how it affects educational practice, we knew that in addition to unpacking the term itself and its effects on us as human being and educators, we also wanted to highlight the work of practitioners whose own sense of urgency has led them to create instructional opportunities that focus on how fake news affects their learners. We'll let their stories speak for themselves, but first some context: We've decided to present these interviews without any interference from us. You'll see information that each teacher provided as they presented it to us, beneath the questions that we posed to them. We think there's a lot to be learned from their experiences, and as you read, we encourage you to consider the following questions:

- What parallels can you draw between the experiences of these educators and your own?
- How have these practitioners faced the challenge of approaching sensitive topics (such as politics) with young people?
- What aspects of their work can you apply to your own?

Arika Dickens: Librarian, London, England

Currently, Arika Dickens is the lower school (PK–4) librarian at ACS Hillingdon International School in London, England.

Why Did You Feel Tackling This Topic with Your Students Was Necessary?

The phrase *fake news* is pretty common, even for my internationally educated and worldly fourth graders. All had heard it and were intrigued by how they could learn to spot it. They didn't know, though, the context of the word *fake*. Was fake news only news that was a lie, or could it be more than that?

As we had access to technology (we are a 1:1 iPad school), there was no reason not to teach students website analysis and evaluation skills along with basics in internet searching, which is the backbone of spotting fake news. Knowing my students were mostly age nine, however, I had to keep the lessons highly engaging and age-appropriate.

Can You Outline Your Approach or Lessons?

With student interest and engagement paramount in the topic of fake news, I turned to literature, using the book *Two Truths and a Lie* by Ammi-Joan Paquette and Laurie Ann Thompson as the backbone of our unit. This engaging, age-appropriate book challenges students to separate fact from fiction through topics about the natural world.

Prior to sharing the text, I asked students if they knew the basis of the game Two Truths and a Lie. Most did, so I gave three examples from my life, and they had to guess which was the lie. One of my examples—"I was named after my great-great-great uncle Arik, a Viking"—could be identified as a lie using some simple sleuthing. Students in two of three classes knew a bit about Viking history and when they lived to give evidence that my lie was being named after a great-great-great uncle. (He would've been a far-distant uncle!) This was the springboard to the lesson: using knowledge that could be confirmed (hopefully, in multiple sources) to identify truths and lies.

The gist of the lessons was:

- **Week 1:** I read a chapter aloud, displaying it on our teaching screen so students could see the detailed images, captions, and text. While I read, students had a note-taking template. I modeled identifying keywords and wrote down my keywords. They were able to use my keywords or write their own; most did a mix.

- **Week 2:** This was web-searching week, and students used keywords to locate websites that confirmed or didn't support the stories shared. After twenty to thirty minutes of work time (this could be independent or in small groups), the class came together for a guided lesson in using keywords; navigating search results; using tabs, such as News, to filter results; and so on. Using their searches as the springboard, we explored what they found online and how they found it (for example, Boolean searches or using quotes to group words). During this time, I implicitly taught them to look at website names and article authors, dates of publication, and image sources. Our whole-class discussion included verifying information on multiple websites by reputable authors.

- **Weeks 3 and 4:** After two weeks, there was so much student interest that we continued for another two weeks using a different chapter of *Two Truths and a Lie* as research inspiration.

- **Conclusion:** The unit concluded with classes creating short videos sharing what they'd learned in online searching and identifying fake news using images from their web searches. This culminating activity was possible because the school is 1:1 iPad.

What Stood Out After the Lesson or Unit?

Three things stood out:

- The need to verify information on more than one trustworthy page
- The importance of looking at a website's address
- The usefulness of the toolbar underneath the search box in Google

Students also learned to click News in the Google toolbar to limit searches to news websites. Here are more of their reflections on what they learned in their own words:

- "We found out that a good way to search was by adding quotes to it."

- "Wikipedia is a good place to check as long as you can guarantee it by checking with other places [on the internet]. But if you can't, then anybody can change it, and that's not good when you're looking [online]."

- "We looked at different websites to confirm if it's real or if it's false."

- "A tip for using this book is when you search up what you want to know about, you go to the section 'News' to figure out everything you can. Here, when I searched up 'tiny dragon olm,' it gives us a lot of very trustworthy websites about the olms." [Her video showed her pointing out each news website and the News tab.]

- "Some things I learned about Wikipedia is that it can give you very useful information, and it is also made by different people."

- "Another way to tell is by looking at who made the website. The person who discovered the Pacific Northwest Tree Octopus was named Zapato, and this website is named zapatopi.net. So, it might not be very trustworthy. So you should look at two websites before you decide something."

- "Here's a way you can tell if it's fake news: by looking up here [pointing to the web address] or by looking at more than one website. If two of them say the same thing and the third one says something different, it's probably fake news."

Do You Have Any Tips for Educators?

As I had multiple students who were new to English and needing extra support, modeling and offering small group work options was vital. During independent research time, I worked with students who needed additional support on forming keyword searches and analyzing and evaluating websites.

What Responses Did You Receive from Students, Parents, Teachers, Administrators?

Students enjoyed this unit so much they wanted to continue researching! They were shocked that headlines don't always speak the truth. They really responded to using quotation marks to search for an exact phrase.

Administrators and teachers in different divisions were very pleased and astonished by the depth of student learning with this unit. They were surprised that this was something that would be taught in a lower school library, yet they thought the way it was taught—using the book to facilitate searches—was innovative. As it turns out, the unit has continued to be mentioned as an exemplar unit of digital literacy by our tech department since I taught it in November and December of 2017.

As this is an international school, I rarely see parents. However, because we use Seesaw to share work and newsletters, I shared photos of our learning and the students' reflection videos. One parent wrote that *"Two Truths and a Lie* was a huge hit" for her fourth-grade son. Another commented on her child's video, "I am impressed with the way you filter the information. It is a great thing to know as you will always need it." A third said, "All good information [child], and you did a good job explaining it. I'll have to keep those tips in mind for my future searches. Thanks!"

Len Bryan: Library Technical Systems Manager, Denver, Colorado

Len Bryan currently serves as a library technical systems manager for Denver Public Schools. Previously, he taught in Hillsboro, Oregon, at four high schools, four middle schools, two alternative schools, and twenty-five elementary schools. He has also taught English for Grades 6–12, coached athletics, and served as a school librarian at middle school, high school, district, and state levels.

Why Did You Feel Tackling This Topic with Your Students Was Necessary?

Joyce Valenza's blog post, "Truth, Truthiness, Triangulation: A News Literacy Toolkit for a 'Post-Truth' World" (November 26, 2016) came at the perfect time. I, along with most of the rest of the country, was in a major funk following the 2016 U.S. presidential election, wondering what was going to happen to our country, and what in the world I could do, aside from fleeing to Canada. I knew that students (as well as adults) were having major problems in filtering real information from partisan noise, and that a basic misunderstanding of media literacy was largely to blame for the mess in which we found ourselves. As a political centrist, I saw blame on both side of the political divide (and have for a very long time). I felt a civic responsibility to do my part to help our teachers and students learn that there is a place for news literacy in social studies, English, and in many other courses, and that it is part of a vital skill set for the survival of our democracy. Add my desire to advance civil discourse among our society, and my never-ending search for engaging materials to present to teachers, and in turn, to students—fake news and media literacy was a no-brainer in terms of the next topic for me to tackle.

Can You Outline Your Approach or Lessons?

The good news is that the teachers I first presented this to were very receptive to the idea of explicitly teaching information and news literacy. They had the usual questions, such as "How will we fit this in?" My recommendation depended on their subject. For social studies teachers, we compared propaganda from World War II to modern propaganda from political action committees, candidates, and political parties in the recent election. This comparison focused on the types of mis- and disinformation used in both propaganda and political advertising, appealing to emotions instead of reason. For English teachers, news and information literacy lends itself to a ton of Common Core State Standards, including author's purpose, language, word choice, tone, and more.

I first presented news literacy at a professional development session for teachers, then was invited into about a dozen or so classrooms in a couple of our high schools over the next two semesters to present the lesson to students directly. We reviewed and took a quick, fun Kahoot! quiz on news literacy vocabulary, then dug into some mis- and disinformation techniques. (You can access Len's Kahoot! quiz here: bit.ly/2KBIgHa.)

We then analyzed some of the "news" articles found on the extreme left and right side of Vanessa Otero's "Media Bias Chart" (see Table 6.1) to orient ourselves with some of the techniques highly biased sources tend to employ.

What Stood Out After the Lesson or Unit?

Students enjoyed critically analyzing some of the same articles their family and friends had shared on social media as fact and were able to have very serious, mature conversations about their findings.

I found the kids were more open-minded about their beliefs than many adults!

Do You Have Any Tips for Educators?

I'd like to expand this learning in upcoming years to include memes and other popular, brief forms of information.

I think being conversant around media literacy and sharing some of that knowledge with students and teachers has opened up some collaborative doors that I may not have had a chance to use otherwise, especially in working with social studies teachers. English has always been the librarian's go-to department, and embracing the fake news phenomenon as a teachable moment has helped me break out of that rut.

What Responses Did You Receive from Students, Parents, Teachers, Administrators?

Teachers were enthusiastic about having this conversation with students and enjoyed having a "guest speaker" come in and work with them. The students were really engaged, especially since we were working with very current events.

Bill Ferriter: Teacher, Apex, North Carolina

Bill Ferriter is a sixth-grade classroom teacher in Apex, North Carolina. You can find him on Twitter @plugusin.

Why Did You Feel Tackling This Topic with Your Students Was Necessary?

I feel strongly that literacy has to include developing the skills to be a discerning, responsible citizen in an increasingly complex world. That has to include being able to identify sources of reliable—and unreliable—information.

Can You Outline Your Approach or Lessons?

For my sixth-grade students, I try to keep things simple. I ask students to think about the following three questions:

- How believable is this story to me?
- What do I know about this news source?
- Can I spot any loaded words or images in this piece?

I emphasize those three questions because they create an easy filter that students can apply without tons of effort. That means they are more likely to get in the regular habit of deliberately evaluating the quality of the news sources that they are examining. If I create a more complicated process for evaluating news sources, students would be less likely to use it on a regular basis. Nothing here is hard for kids to do.

I also like that the questions emphasize common sense as a filter for judging the reliability of news sources. That's the primary tool that responsible citizens should always use when determining whether something is believable or not, and it encourages skepticism—something that is healthy when working with information in an increasingly biased world.

Teaching these skills hasn't been hard either. I share intentionally biased articles with students in class three or four times per quarter, let students know that those articles are biased in advance, and ask them to spot evidence of that bias in action. The lessons take me less than ten minutes in total, which means I'm more likely to keep teaching them. Frequency becomes the essential factor for reinforcing the core notion that fake news is a real problem that students need to be aware of.

What Responses Did You Receive from Students, Parents, Teachers, Administrators?

Middle school kids love these lessons. They are always shocked at first that people "get away" with publishing fake news on the internet. Then, they feel strongly that the authors are "being unfair," and that bugs them. Once they know that they have a set of easy tools for "fighting back," they become determined to use them. They see it as an issue of justice: catching liars and preventing others from being tricked.

I think that's neat. If we can tap into that commitment to information fairness and honesty when kids are young, my hope is that they will remain committed to those same principles when they get older.

Do You Have Any Tips for Educators?

The biggest advice that I'd offer is, "Get started! Now."

Fake news is a real problem in our world. People are intentionally manipulating the thinking of others, and that's frightening. Democracies depend on an educated populace; we've always known that. Unfortunately, the information that we have access to is increasingly unreliable. We can't make good decisions as people unless we prepare kids to sift through the misinformation that surrounds them.

On the Front Lines

We are inspired by the work of practitioners, such as Arika, Len, and Bill, who aren't waiting for their local curricula to catch up with the needs of students. Instead, these teachers and librarians, like countless others, are charging ahead and crafting meaningful instructional opportunities for learners of all ages, to help prepare them for a world in which media literacy is more important than ever.

Even though each of the three educators we profiled works with students in different corners of the world and in different situations, you likely spotted some of the same commonalities we did. The most glaring is the sense of urgency that guides their work. We can relate with Len when he says he felt "a civic responsibility to do my part to help our teachers and students learn that there is a place for new literacy in social studies, English, and in many other courses, and that it is part of a vital skill set for the survival of our democracy." Like Len, Arika, and Bill, we feel called to action by events around the world and in our backyards, and we admire greatly the teachers on the front lines whose work is producing outcomes that will affect us all. We may not be able to change the number of lily pads in the pond, or, in this case, the number of creators of fake news, but these educators are proving that we *can* change the way our students evaluate the information they find online. We *can* change the way we think about media literacy as a part of core instruction. And we *can* make our work part of what changes the environment in which those lily pads currently thrive.

Chapter 7

1. What parallels were you able to draw between the experiences of these educators and your own? What aspects of their work can you apply to your own?

2. In what ways could the lessons shared by each of the educators in this chapter be adapted to include the use of mobile devices? And how might you implement these changes with students in an environment where not everyone has access to a mobile device?

3. Tweet us! What's one question you have for one (or more) of the educators profiled in this chapter? Tweet them your questions or shout outs, and don't forget to include the #factvsfiction hashtag!

CHAPTER 8

Critical Thinking Now More Than Ever

If you logged into Facebook in early April of 2017, you were likely greeted by a notification alerting you to Facebook's new "Tips to Spot False News" (Costine, 2017). Although this notification appeared for a few days only, it was part of several steps the social media giant took, including providing ways for users to report suspect stories being shared on the network, to combat a problem its founder Mark Zuckerberg first denied even existed (Shahani, 2016). As we watched these new resources for social media users roll out, we noted with interest that although certainly some work was being done behind the scenes to delete automated accounts and the monetary incentives behind them, the onus remained primarily on users to establish better strategies for determining fact from fiction online—and to report it when they spotted it.

Interestingly, this strategy mirrors our own feelings about what will ultimately be the solution to the media literacy crisis we are currently facing. A 2017 Pew Research Center poll asked respondents to predict whether or not in the next ten years the information landscape would change in a way that made it more difficult for misleading/biased information to spread. The results were nearly evenly split, with 51% of people reporting that they did not believe the internet would be a better place for truth seekers in the next decade (Anderson & Rainie, 2017). Both those who were optimistic about the future and those were not agreed on one thing, however: The outcome would be the result of the people *using* those networks, not those creating them. In short, whether we succeed or fail at making our information-rich world one in which truth prevails is entirely up to us. Which is, of course, where you come in.

Educators: Kryptonite to Fake News

When we work with educators, our discussions surrounding the topic of fake news typically focus around three central concerns:

- It's difficult to teach students to be media literate when so many of their teachers' social media feeds are flooded with fake news stories, propaganda, and highly biased materials.

- It's difficult to teach students about fake news, because we simply don't have time, and the approaches are not tested.

- It's difficult to teach students about fake news without bringing up politics—a topic that can make educators uncomfortable or afraid of backlash from parents, administrators, or both.

Let's look at each concern a bit more closely.

Do as We Say, Not as We Do

How can we effectively nurture media literacy, when our own news feeds are flooded with propaganda, biased material, and other fake news? We can't. Asking students to do as we say but not as we do is a recipe for disaster. Remember, the resources shared in this book aren't just good for students. They can also be useful in helping other educators assess and sharpen their own media literacy skills, which are increasingly also citizenship skills. We encourage building-level administrators to replicate the tasks posed to students in the Stanford History Education Group's media literacy study with teachers during a faculty meeting or professional development opportunity (see Chapter 6 for more details). Regardless of the outcomes, we predict highly informative results.

Jennifer created a lengthy Breakout-EDU experience (Figure 8.1) for teachers surrounding fake news, media literacy, and what we can all do as educators to support students as digital citizens in a world where we can't always trust the information we find online.

Using both digital and physical BreakoutEDU strategies, this experience immerses teachers in resources to help them both hone their own skills and discover new strategies to use with students. Educators who have participated in this professional development come away with similar responses reflecting the fundamental truth: We have a lot of

Figure 8.1 Unlock skills to foil fake news! BreakoutEDU can be used for staff, too.

work to do, but we can do it! Free for you to use or replicate, this resource is available at www.librarygirl.net. You'll also find an answer key, as well as a resource list to help you adapt or replicate the experience for your staff or professional learning community (PLC).

Fair or not, as educators, we are often seen as leaders in our communities. What we post online should reflect examples of how social media can be a positive tool for connecting with other people and for sharing information that contributes productively to our collective knowledge. Although some districts' social media policies may state otherwise, we do not feel teachers have an obligation to remain politically neutral. We *do* believe that if we choose to share information online that conveys our political (or other) beliefs, educators absolutely *do* have a responsibility to make certain that those posts contain vetted, verifiable resources.

Untested Teaching Amid Time Constraints

On his blog, *The Tempered Radical*, North Carolina teacher Bill Ferriter wrote,

> We don't need new policies and tools from tech companies to identify sketchy content on the web. Instead we need to develop citizens who take careful steps to verify that the information they are reading anywhere on the web is reliable. That's the new literacy in today's complicated media ecology—and it is the new literacy that we give too little attention to in schools. (2016)

Although this is true, it's not because information literacy isn't mentioned in the standards. Both the ISTE Standards for Students and the Common Core State Standards for Literacy speak specifically to skills necessary for media literacy (Figure 8.2).

These standards, along with similar language in many state standards, can be leveraged, if necessary, to defend devoting time to teaching media literacy in your classes. But beyond that, you must be brave in your belief that:

- Not all instruction has to look like the test in order to prepare students for the test.
- Although preparing students to do well on that single, highly emphasized day is an important part of your job, preparing them for all the days before it and for all the days after, is a job that matters much more.

Uncomfortable Topics

Concerns about backlash from parents and administrators over sensitive topics are real, and we're not dismissing them. However, as we saw in Chapter 7, there are examples of how to approach these topics with students in ways that require respectful dialogue and that focus on source, rather than personal, credibility. The world is full of uncomfortable topics, and we all have to make judgments about the appropriate time and place to have these difficult discussions with young people. But, we can't teach kids to make good choices without actually *giving them choices*. Put another way, if

2B **Communicate information and ideas** effectively to multiple audiences using a variety of media and formats.

3B Locate, organize, analyze, **evaluate, synthesize, and ethically use information from a variety of sources and media.**

3C **Evaluate and select information sources** and digital tools based on the appropriateness to specific tasks.

From the ISTE Standards for Students (2016). For complete Standards, visit: https://www.iste.org/ standards/for-students

CCSS.ELA-LITERACY.RH.6-8.6
Identify aspects of a text that reveal an **author's point of view or purpose** (e.g., loaded language, inclusion, or avoidance of particular facts).

CCSS.ELA-LITERACY.RH.6-8.8
Distinguish among fact, opinion, and reasoned judgment in a text.

CCSS.ELA-LITERACY.RH.11-12.8
Evaluate an **author's premises, claims, and evidence** by corroborating or challenging them with other information.

CCSS.ELA-LITERACY.RI.7.6
Determine an **author's point of view or purpose** in a text and analyze how the author distinguishes his or her **position** from that of others.

CCSS.ELA-LITERACY.RI.7.8
Trace and evaluate the **argument and specific claims** in a text, assessing whether the reasoning is sound and the **evidence is relevant and sufficient** to support the claims.

CCSS.ELA-LITERACY.RI.7.9
Analyze how two or more authors writing about the same topic shape their presentations of key information by emphasizing different evidence or **advancing different interpretations of facts.**

Figure 8.2 Our standards can help us make the case for teaching content that is not tested but that remains critically important.

we don't teach our students how to have civil, respectful conversations with people whose experiences and ideas are different from our own, who will? We already know what it looks like to live in a world in which people show very little respect for each other online (and increasingly in person). If we want our students to be better than we are, we have to teach them how.

What's more, truth is a bipartisan issue. There's no such thing as "alternative facts." The same fact can be used by different people to support alternative opinions, but the facts don't change. Different people can use the same facts to emphasize conflicting ideas or to inform different theories, but the facts remain the same. Facts are non-partisan. Facts alone are neutral. It's what we do with them that becomes biased and controversial. We don't think it's hyperbolic to say that there's a battle being waged between the truth and those who seek to distort it for personal gain. This battle is why conversations about what is actually true and what has been created to look like truth, but which actually seeks to further an agenda, can be painful. When a resource supports or disproves deeply held beliefs, reactions can be charged, even explosive. Plus, because so many of these conversations occur behind the shield of the keyboard, it's easy for things to devolve quickly.

We believe our classrooms and libraries can be safe places for students (and teachers) to learn how to navigate these potential minefields—but only if we step up as defenders of truth. It simply doesn't matter who you voted for or what your stance is on any number of issues. As an educator, you must be a warrior for truth, with your professional practice being the kryptonite to fake news and those who seek to benefit from spreading it.

Let's Do This!

Every year, the web design company Go Globe produces an updated version of its "What Happens Every 60 Seconds on the Internet" infographic. And every year, the results are shocking. In 2017, more than 400 hours of video were uploaded to YouTube every 60 seconds, more than 65,000 new photos were posted to Instagram. More than 250,000 were uploaded to Facebook. That's *every single minute*. The amount of information we are faced with each day is simply staggering. That volume coupled with the way that information is being manipulated for gain or profit can make for an especially daunting task for educators who, ready or not, are on the front lines of this battle.

The resources shared in this book are a good starting point as you rally support for the work ahead. Again, the good news is that you don't have to do it alone. In addition to your teacher-librarians, support is plentiful. Within the mountain of new information that was created while you read this chapter, there will no doubt also be new resources for helping you and your students more deftly navigate it. Moreover, although the tools that enable the exponential connectedness of our lives make this work challenging, they are also the same tools by which we can connect with an army of other warriors in the same battle. The work ahead is difficult. But it is critical. And ultimately, we are optimistic about the outcome, because we believe in the power of educators to change the world.

Chapter 8

1. What's one thing you can do tomorrow to begin the work of preparing your students to navigate a world in which much of the information shared online, in the form of news, shouldn't be taken at face value?

2. You've read this book (and maybe a few others). You've talked with your colleagues and consulted your PLN. You've planned lessons and are ready to move forward. How will you measure success? How will you know that your learners have the skills they need to discern fact from fiction in the information they consume?

3. Tweet us! What lingering questions do you have? What's something you still need to build (a resource, a learning space, a relationship) in order to move forward with this work?

References

Above The Noise. (2018, January 24). *Are internet trolls born or made?* [Video file]. Retrieved from bit.ly/2oljH8b

ALA (Ed.). (2011, August 19). *Banned Websites Awareness Day.* Retrieved from www.ala.org/aasl/advocacy/bwad

Anderson, M., & Jiang, J. (2018, May 31). Teens, social media & technology 2018. Pew Research Center. Retrieved from pewrsr.ch/2onpHwU

Anderson, J., & Rainie, L. (2017, October 19). The future of truth and misinformation online. Pew Research Center. Retrieved from pewrsr.ch/2N6PuYe

Argen, D. (2017, September 21). Frida Sofía, age 12: the Mexico City quake "survivor" who was never there. *The Guardian.* Retrieved from http://bit.ly/2N4ojom

Associated Press. (2018, September 21). Trapped girl's wiggling fingers captivate Mexico after earthquake. NBC News. Retrieved from nbcnews.to/2N4kFDI

Ault, S. (2015, July 23). Digital star popularity grows versus mainstream celebrities. *Variety.* Retrieved from bit.ly/2N1r965

BBC News. (2017, June 25). *Prices for fake news campaigns revealed.* Retrieved from https://www.bbc.com/news/technology-40287399

Ben-Ghiat, R. (2016, August 10). An American authoritarian. *The Atlantic.* Retrieved from bit.ly/2LLTSau

Bialik, K., & Matsa, K. E. (2017, October 4). Key trends in social and digital news media. Pew Research Center. Retrieved from pewrsr.ch/2ojCNLM

Bloomberg. (2018, February 27). Why "success" on YouTube still means a life of poverty. *Fortune.* Retrieved from https://for.tn/2N3vUMK

California State University. (2010, September 17). *Evaluating information—applying the CRAAP test*. Retrieved from http://bit.ly/2N3c7wH

Casad, B. (2016, August 1). Confirmation bias. In *Encyclopedia Britannica online*. Retrieved from bit.ly/2N3keth

Claburn, T. (2017, August 25). Ad blocking basically doesn't exist on mobile. *The Register*. Retrieved from bit.ly/2omApE0

Clickbait. (2018, September 1). In *Merriam-Webster's online dictionary*. Retrieved from https://www.merriam-webster.com/dictionary/clickbait

Conspiracy Theory. (2018, September 1). In *Merriam-Webster's online dictionary*. Retrieved from https://www.merriam-webster.com/dictionary/conspiracy theory

Costine, J. (2017, April 6). Facebook puts link to 10 tips for spotting "false news" atop feed. *Tech Crunch*. Retrieved from https://tcrn.ch/2No4rvs

Cottrell, M. (2016, December 16). Hate incidents in libraries spark a renewed commitment to serve all. *School Library Journal*. Retrieved from bit.ly/2MXBG2t

Crook, J. (2015, February 9). Snapchat selfie at scene of alleged crime is key evidence in murder case. *Tech Crunch*. Retreived from 9 Feb. 2015, tcrn.ch/2N1mKjz

Daly, C. B. (2017, April 28). How Woodrow Wilson's propaganda machine changed American journalism. *Smithsonian*. Retrieved from bit.ly/2onrfqZ

Dator, J. (2016, November 22). Facts don't matter [Cartoon]. *The New Yorker*. Retrieved from https://www.newyorker.com/cartoon/a20602

Daum, M. (2013, March 7). Daum: Online's "nasty effect." *Los Angeles Times*. Retrieved from lat.ms/2NocwA3

Dickinson, T. (2016, December 5). Fake news is lazy language [Tweet]. Retrieved from https://twitter.com/7im

Disinformation. (2018, September 2). In *Merriam-Webster's online dictionary*. Retrieved from https://www.merriam-webster.com/dictionary/disinformation

Duggan, M. (2017, July 11). Online harassment 2017. Pew Research Center. Retrieved from pewrsr.ch/2onb5Oa

Edelman, R. (2018, February 12). *Edelman trust barometer*. Retrieved from https://www.edelman.com//trust-barometer

Elizabeth, J. (2017, July 25). Why Snopes matters. American Press Institute. Retrieved from bit.ly/2N1smu9

Esplin, B. (2016, February 5). The expanding lily pad: A retirement riddle [Blog post]. *The Micawber Principle*. Retrieved from bit.ly/2N6Qwn4

Explorable.com (2010, September 4). *Confirmation bias*. Retrieved from https://explorable.com/confirmation-bias

Ferriter, W. (2016, November 21). What are you doing to teach students to spot fake news stories? [Blog post]. *The Tempered Radical*. Retrieved from bit.ly/2N1ywe4

File, T. (2017, May 10). Voting in America: A look at the 2016 presidential election [Blog post]. Census Blogs. Retrieved from bit.ly/2MZk5a9

Fox, M. (2018, March 8). Fake news: Lies spread faster on social media than truth does. NBC News. Retrieved from nbcnews.to/2NbShzK

GO-Gulf Web Design Company. (2017, August 21). *Things that happen on the internet every 60 seconds* [Infographic]. Retrieved from bit.ly/2okvB23

Green, M. (2017, January 24). No comment! Why more news sites are dumping their comment sections. KQED News. Retrieved from bit.ly/2N3loGH

Gu, L., Kropotov, V., & Yarochkin, F. (2017). The fake news machine how propagandists abuse the internet and manipulate the public. *Micro Trend*. Retrieved from bit.ly/2MZvoAO

Hawkins, D. (2017, June 8). Sandy Hook hoaxer gets prison time for threatening 6-year-old victim's father. *The Washington Post*. Retrieved from wapo.st/2oj81CS

Hawkins-Gaar, K. (2013 April 3) 36 stories that prove citizen journalism matters. CNN. Retrieved from cnn.it/2wzbdOf

History. (2009). *Oklahoma City bombing*. Retrieved from bit.ly/2wyjxxZ

Information. (n.d.). In *Oxford Living Dictionaries*. Retrieved from https://en.oxforddictionaries.com/definition/information

Irving, C. (2018, January 12). Trump's war on the press follows the Mussolini and Hitler playbook. *The Daily Beast*. Retrieved from thebea.st/2NF36ro

Izadi, E. (2017, March 10). Chinese media fooled by Borowitz Report. Is this kind of "satire" okay in a fake-news era? *The Washington Post*. Retrieved from https://wapo.st/2olqcaX.

Knight, J. L. (2016, May 11). News goes mobile: How people use smartphones to access information. *Medium*. Retrieved from bit.ly/2onHXXe

Kolbert, E. (2017, February 2). Why facts don't change our minds. *The New Yorker*. Retrieved from bit.ly/2N4gWWw

LaGarde, J. (2011, July 25). Librarians are ready. Are you? [Blog post]. *The Adventures of Library Girl*. Retrieved from bit.ly/2MZ5fR4

Lance, K. C. (2014, February 11). The impact of school librarians and library programs on academic achievement of student [Blog post]. *Keith Curry Lance*. Retrieved from bit.ly/2olIJ72

Lance, K. C. (2018, March 16). School librarian, where art thou? *School Library Journal*. Retrieved from bit.ly/2N8KWAZ

Leswing, K. (2018, April 3). Facebook is finally launching a new feature to combat fake news, after six months of testing—here's how it works. *Business Insider*. Retrieved from read.bi/2N1sOsl

Lewis, P. (2018, February 2). "Fiction is outperforming reality:" How YouTube's algorithm distorts truth. *The Guardian*. Retrieved from bit.ly/2MZKOU9

Lindberg, M. (2016, November 28). The Trump effect: The impact of the 2016 presidential election on our nation's schools. Southern Poverty Law Center. Retrieved from bit.ly/2onc54S

Madden, M., Lenhart, A., & Fontaine, C. (2017, February). How youth navigate the news landscape. Knight Foundation. Retrieved from bit.ly/2No5taO

Markham, T. (2016, November 16). Why empathy holds the key to transforming 21st century learning. NPR. Retrieved from bit.ly/2ojFeoS

Meserole, C., & Polyakova, A. (2018, May 25). The West is ill-prepared for the wave of "deep fakes" that artificial intelligence could unleash. Brookings Institution. Retrieved from https://brook.gs/2N1im4l

Morton, B. A., & Dalton, B. (2007). Changes in instructional hours in four subjects by public school teachers of grades 1 through 4. *Stats In Brief, 2007*(305). Retrieved from https://nces.ed.gov/pubs2007/2007305.pdf

Mullany, G. (2017, September 21). No child trapped in rubble of Mexican quake-hit school, officials say. *The New York Times*. Retrieved from nyti.ms/2N4qpx6

Nazi Propaganda. (2016, May 10). In *Holocaust Encyclopedia*. Retrieved from bit.ly/2ondiJs

National Center for Educational Statistics. (2017). *Back to school fast facts*. Retrieved from bit.ly/2MZL71f

National Center for Fair and Open Testing (Ed.). (2007, October). *New evidence strengthens claim that testing narrows curriculum.* Retrieved from bit.ly/2olY3R3

National Historical Publications & Records Commission [NHPRC]. (n.d.). From Benjamin Franklin to [Richard Price], 13 June 1782. National Archives Retrieved from bit.ly/2wxgwPj

National Historical Publications & Records Commission [NHPRC]. (n.d.). Supplement to the Boston Independent Chronicle, [before 22 April 1782]. *National Archives,* Retrieved from bit.ly/2wxgwPj

Newcomb, A. (2018, February 22). How Parkland's social media-savvy teens took back the internet—and the gun control debate. NBC News. Retrieved from nbcnews.to/2MYgtW4

NewseumED. (2017, May). *Is this story share-worthy? Flowchart.* Retrieved from bit.ly/2I2CUD5

Noticieros Televisacom. (2017, September 21). In *Facebook* [Group page]. Retrieved from bit.ly/2olpyKt

Noel, A. (2017, September 21). Mexicans outraged after praying for fake "trapped child." *The Daily Beast.* Retrieved from https://thebea.st/2 Newrvg

NOTIMEX. (2017, September 21). Frida, la perrita que busca sobrevivientes tras el sismo. Retrieved from bit.ly/2onuXAE

November, A. (1995). Teaching Zack to think. November Learning. Retrieved from bit.ly/2N1zs24

November, A. & Mull, B. (2012, October 18). Why more schools aren't teaching web literacy—and how they can start. November Learning. Retrieved from bit.ly/2NicgMZ

Ortero, V. (2018, June 7). Junk food and junk news: The case for "information fitness." Ad Fontes Media. Retrieved from bit.ly/2N2ubXS

Parkinson, R. G. (2016, November 25). Fake News? That's a very old story. *The New York Times.* Retrieved from wapo.st/2LH5jAk

Perrin, A. & Jiang, J. (2018, March 14). About a quarter of U.S. adults say they are "almost constantly" online. Pew Research Center. Retrieved from pewrsr.ch/2N2vEgQ

Persio, S. L. (2017, September 22). Mexico earthquake: Who is Frida Sofia? Mexican authorities just don't know. *Newsweek.* Retrieved from bit.ly/2N3CJxN

Pew Research Center. (2017, May 9). *Use of mobile devices for news continues to grow*. Retrieved from pewrsr.ch/2NoenVx

Pew Research Center. (2018, February 27). *Majority of Americans now use Facebook, YouTube*. Retrieved from pewrsr.ch/2otkrbv

Post-Truth. (n.d.). In *Oxford Living Dictionaries*. Retrieved from bit. ly/2omXnep

Printing Press. (2018, June 10). In *Wikipedia*. Retrieved from https://en.wikipedia.org/wiki/Printing_press

Propaganda. (2018, August 27). In *Merriam-Webster's online dictionary*. Retrieved from https://www.merriam-webster.com/dictionary/propaganda

Qiu, X., Oliveira, D., Shirazi, A. S., Flammini, A., & Menczer, F. (2017). Limited individual attention and online virality of low-quality information. *Nature Human Behavior, 1*(0132). Retrieved from https://go.nature.com/2LCCJAj

Robb, A. (2017, November 16). Anatomy of a fake news scandal. *Rolling Stone Magazine*. Retrieved from rol.st/2onuVJj

Satire. (2018, August 8). In *Merriam-Webster's online dictionary*. Retrieved from https://www.merriam-webster.com/dictionary/satire

Satire Examples. (2018, March 28). In *Your Dictionary*. Retrieved from examples.yourdictionary.com/satire-examples.html

Semple, K., Villegas, P., & Malkin, E. (2017, September 19). Mexico earthquake kills hundreds, trapping many under rubble. *The New York Times*. Retrieved from nyti.ms/2wBEoQH

Shahani, A. (2016, November 11). Zuckerberg denies fake news on Facebook had impact on the election. NPR. Retrieved from n.pr/2omECaM

Shane, S. (2018, September 7). The fake Americans Russia created to influence the election. *The New York Times*. Retrieved from nyti.ms/2MXDeJP

Shapiro, J. (2016, September 9). How to train 68.8 million teachers. Because that's how many the world needs. *Forbes*. Retrieved from bit.ly/2No7Uds

Shearer, E. & Gottfried, J. (2017, September 7). News use across social media platforms 2017. Pew Research Center. Retrieved from pewrsr.ch/2oobVua

Silver, K. (2017, September 9). Beware of Social media during terror events, NHS guidelines warn. BBC News. Retrieved from bbc.in/2Ndkt5j

Silverman, C. (2016, November 16). This analysis shows how viral fake election news stories outperformed real news on Facebook. *BuzzFeed News*. Retrieved from bit.ly/2N1k1a5

Silverman, C. (2017, December 28). These are 50 of the biggest fake news hits on Facebook in 2017. *BuzzFeed News*. Retrieved from bit.ly/2N3Z1iO

Smith, A., & Banic, V. (2016, December 9). Fake news: How a partying Macedonian teen earns thousands publishing lies. NBC News. Retrieved from nbcnews.to/2onNAVs

Soares, I. (2017, September 13). The fake news machine. CNN Money. Retrieved from cnnmon.ie/2olKPnq

Specia, M. (2017, September 27). "Frida Sofia:" The Mexico earthquake victim who never was. *The New York Times*. Retrieved from https://nyti.ms/2olKQYw

Special Report. (2018, January 25). Waging war with disinformation. *The Economist*. Retrieved from econ.st/2om04g5

Stanford History Education Group. (2016, November 22). *Evaluating information: The cornerstone of civic online reasoning.* Retrieved from stanford.io/2olraUx

Steinberg, L. (2017, July 26). Beyond fake news—10 types of misleading news. EAVI. Retrieved from bit.ly/2omFdcw

Steinmetz, K. (2018, August 9). How your brain tricks you into believing fake news. *Time*. Retrieved from ti.me/2NCT3Cw

Stelter, B. (2018, January 17). Trump averages a "fake" insult every day. Really. We counted. CNN Money. Retrieved from cnnmon.ie/2MYh8H2

Straus, V. (2015, March 10). No child left behind: What standardized test scores reveal about its legacy. *The Washington Post*. Retrieved from wapo.st/2MZnaqJ

Storr, W. (2015). *The unpersuadables: Adventures with the enemies of science.* New York, NY: Overlook Press.

Stroud, N. J., & Gomez, L. (2017, June 8). *Snapchat survey shows that distrust in the media is not so simple.* Retrieved from bit.ly/snapchat_survey

Survey [By J. LaGarde & D. Hudgins]. (2018, March 6). Retrieved from https://goo.gl/forms/G8vxY5NdoU33Zbey2

Tavernise, S. (2016, December 6). As fake news spreads lies, more readers shrug at the truth. *The New York Times*. Retrieved from nyti.ms/2MZnxBD

The Onion. (2018, January 25). In *Wikipedia*. Retrieved from https://en.wikipedia.org/wiki/The_Onion

The Only Thing Necessary for the Triumph of Evil Is that Good Men Do Nothing. (2010). *Quote Investigator*. Retrieved from bit.ly/2MXr17V

Townsend, R. B. (2007, July 30). "No child" leaves the social studies behind. *Perspectives on History*. Retrieved from bit.ly/2MZMbCh

United States Holocaust Memorial Museum. (n.d.). Introduction to the Holocaust. *Holocaust Encyclopedia*. Retrieved from bit.ly/2ondiJs

Valenza, J. (2016, November 26). Truth, truthiness, triangulation: A news literacy toolkit for a "post-truth" world. *School Library Journal*. Retrieved from bit.ly/2N3z4QC

Volmiero, J. (2017, September 21). Rescue dog Frida is assisting relief efforts in Mexico following massive earthquake. *Global News*. Retrieved from bit.ly/2Nl9ZRg

Wineburg, S. & McGrew, S. (2016, November 1). Why students can't google their way to the truth. *Education Week*. Retrieved from bit.ly/2MS9PBn

Wintour, P. (2017, November 28). "Fake news:" Libya seizes on Trump tweet to discredit CNN slavery report. *The Guardian*. Retrieved from bit.ly/2N74NR2

Woolf, N. (2016, November 17). As fake news takes over Facebook feeds, many are taking satire as fact. *The Guardian*. Retrieved from bit.ly/2onMoBm

Word of the Year. (n.d.). In *Oxford Living Dictionaries*. Retrieved from bit.ly/2N2Xbid

Zielezinski, M. (2016, May 19). *What a decade of education research tells us about technology in the hands of underserved students*. Retrieved from bit.ly/2aHo6va

Zapato, L. (2018, May 22). *The Pacific Northwest Tree Octopus*. Retrieved from https://zapatopi.net/treeoctopus

Index

Your opinion matters: Tell us how we're doing!

Your feedback helps ISTE create the best possible resources for teaching and learning in the digital age. Share your thoughts with the community or tell us how we're doing!

You can:

- Write a review at amazon.com or barnesandnoble.com.
- Mention this book on social media and follow ISTE on Twitter @iste, Facebook @ISTEconnects or Instagram @isteconnects.
- Email us at books@iste.org with your questions or comments.